THE DIGITAL WORLD

DIGITAL VIDEO
MOVING IMAGES AND COMPUTERS

01000010110
11000011100
10110001011
11011011010
00110010100
00011000011
01000010110
11000011100
10110001011
11011011010
00110010100
00011000011
01000010110
11000011100
10110001011

THE DIGITAL WORLD

THE DIGITAL WORLD

DIGITAL VIDEO
MOVING IMAGES AND COMPUTERS

01000010110
11000011100
10110001011
11011011010
00110010100
00011000011
01000010110
11000011100
10110001011
11011011010
00110010100
00011000011
01000010110
11000011100
10110001011

ANANDA MITRA, PH.D.

CHELSEA HOUSE
PUBLISHERS
An imprint of Infobase Publishing

Digital Video: Moving Images and Computers

Chelsea House
An imprint of Infobase Publishing
132 West 31st Street
New York NY 10001

Library of Congress Cataloging-in-Publication Data
Mitra, Ananda, 1960–
   Digital video : moving images and computers / Ananda Mitra.
     p. cm. — (The digital world. Digital communications)
   Includes bibliographical references and index.
   ISBN 978-0-8160-6792-3 (hardcover)
   1. Digital video—Juvenile literature.   I. Title.   II. Series.

   TK6680.5.M58 2010
   006.6'96—dc22
                                                       2009052503

Text design by Annie O'Donnell
Cover design by Keith Trego
Composition by Newgen North America
Cover printed by Bang Printing, Brainerd, MN
Book printed and bound by Bang Printing, Brainerd, MN
Date printed: June 2010
Printed in the United States of America

10 9 8 7 6 5 4 3 2 1

This book is printed on acid-free paper.

Contents

Preface

These days, it is not unusual for 10- to 12-year-olds to be publishing their own Web sites or for second and third graders to begin computer classes. At the same time, computer games are becoming increasingly popular as major publishing houses continue to churn out educational computer programs for children in preschool. At the other end of the spectrum, technological know-how has become a requirement for most jobs in an increasingly digital world, as the computer has become a common tool in most professions. Even the often-mentioned "digital divide" between those who have access to computers and those who do not is being bridged with the development of tools such as the XD computer designed by the Massachusetts Institute of Technology Media Laboratory and the availability of computers at libraries and schools. As people become more reliant on digital devices to perform everyday tasks, these modern conveniences become commonplace.

Even though there are many different kinds of computers available for everyday use—ranging from gadgets like the BlackBerry to specially made computers for playing computer games—all the machines operate on the fundamental system of ones and zeros called binary, invented in the seventeenth century. Although it might appear that computers and newly developed digital products are "new" technologies, the seeds of modern digital technologies were planted nearly three centuries ago and grew with the research of legendary scholars and engineers such as Gottfried Leibniz and others.

The relevance of digital technologies in everyday life often has been overshadowed by market-driven hype about new technologies that appear to be introduced at a breakneck speed, which leaves so many people scrambling to catch up to the latest gadget. This result, however, is the surface representation of deeper changes in society that are taking place with the adoption of digital tools in different aspects of everyday life. THE DIGITAL WORLD is a set of volumes that aims to explore the whole spectrum of applications, describing how digital systems influence society and helping readers understand the nature of digital systems and their many interacting parts. The set covers major applications of digital systems and includes the following titles:

- *Digital Communications*
- *Digital Games*
- *Digital Music*
- *Digital Research*
- *Digital Security*
- *Digital Video*

Each volume in the set explores a wide range of material, explains the basic concepts of these applications, and then discusses the implications they have on everyday life. Because the number of possible topics is practically limitless, we focus on a sample of the most interesting and useful applications and tools and explain the basic principles of technology. Readers are encouraged to continue exploring the digital world with the guidance of our Further Resources section featured in each volume. The goal of these books is to encourage the reader to see the relevance of digital systems in all aspects of life, at the present time as well as in the past and in the years to come.

Acknowledgments

I would like to thank a group of people who made this book possible. My thanks first goes to my family in America and India who provided support and balance to my writing life. Appreciation also goes to my friends in Winston-Salem and colleagues at Wake Forest University who provided the encouragement throughout the entire process of doing the six books in this series. Thanks also goes to Elizabeth Oakes for providing photographs that illustrate the different components of the digital world and to Jodie Rhodes, who helped me overcome more than one challenge. Finally, I thank the editors for their patience and encouragement to ensure we create a worthy product. General thanks goes to the publisher for giving me this opportunity.

Moving Images

In 2007, 1.3 billion movie tickets were sold in the United States for the nearly 750 movies released that year. Since Georges Méliès's 1902 experimental film *A Trip to the Moon,* movies have become one of the most important forms of mass entertainment worldwide. The development of television and video technology also provides additional forms of entertainment using moving images.

Artists have long been able to paint or draw still images of the world around them; however, capturing movement and then displaying that image has been a more difficult task. India and China were the first to attempt to display motion by performing "shadow plays." This activity, which is an ancient form of storytelling, involves using a lantern and puppets to display moving shadows on a wall. This form of entertainment spread to Europe in the mid-eighteenth century when French missionaries in China brought it back to France in 1767. It caused quite a stir in the French cities of Paris and Marseilles.

In 1889, William Dickson, an employee of Thomas Edison, invented the Kinetoscope, the first device to show motion pictures. On May 20, 1891, the first demonstration of the device was given at Edison's lab for 150 members of the National Federation of Women's Clubs. Looking through the eyepiece at the top of the machine, the viewer saw about 20 seconds of film. Later, Kinetoscope parlors opened in New York in 1894.

Elsewhere in the world, others began to develop ways to capture moving images. It was in the late 1800s that Thomas Edison and his employees developed the Kinetoscope, a cabinet with a window through which people could view films. The Kinetoscope became the model for all cinematic projection until video. The Lumière brothers of Besançon, France, were also among the earliest film-makers. Auguste and Louis Lumière developed the *cinematographe* system, a three-in-one device that could record, develop, and project moving images. The brothers made it possible to display motion by using a series of still pictures that would either be seen through a viewing hole—like the Kinetoscope—or projected onto a surface.

In both cases, the basic principles of capturing and displaying motion were the same. They were based on the fact that the eye and the brain perceive motion if still pictures are seen in rapid succession with a moment of darkness between each image in the series. The two factors that allow for motion to be perceived are the rate at which the still images are viewed and the need for the moment of darkness between each image. Each image had to be just a little bit different from the one before it and so, all together, they displayed an object that was moving.

The most popular theory that explains the way the brain perceives motion by looking at a series of still images is called *persistence of vision*. This theory claims that the human brain holds on to the memory of an image for a few moments. If a nearly identical image is shown before the memory of the first one is lost, then the still images blend together to produce the illusion of motion. It is generally agreed that if the human eye sees 24 images per second with a dark spot between each frame, then an image of movement would be perceived by the brain.

Psychologists and physiologists have also proposed other explanations about the way in which motion is perceived. The key to the alternative argument lies in understanding how the human eye and brain perceive motion in real life. Experiments demonstrate that the perception of motion as seen on a movie or television screen is

(continues on page 16)

OPTICAL ILLUSIONS

A person's sense of vision is made up of his or her eyes and brain cells. There are instances when the vision system makes a person see things that are actually not real. This results in an optical illusion, with the eye and brain being tricked by certain combinations of light and shade. The brain plays a significant role in interpreting what the eye sees. When a person's brain cells read the signals from the eye in an incorrect fashion, the person sees an optical illusion. Optical illusions fall into four major categories based on the interaction between the way in which the eye operates and the role of the brain in the perception of light and shade.

First, there are *physiological illusions.* In these cases, the excessive stimulation of the eye or the brain misleads the visual system. Many optical illusions take advantage of physiological phenomena by alternating different colors or shapes and overstimulating the brain. This is the basis of the process of perception of vision, which creates the illusion of motion out of a series of still images.

Another general form of optical illusion is called *cognitive illusion.* These do not necessarily overstimulate the optic system, but instead take advantage of the fact that the brain makes unconscious conclusions about what the eye sees. There is a strong cultural aspect to this form of optical illusion, because it is based on one's knowledge of the surrounding world. The illusion is produced by taking advantage of that knowledge. Most often these are illusions that offer an image that might have multiple images built into it. The viewer switches between seeing the different images, while feeling unsure about what the picture exactly represents. For example, silhouettes of two face profiles looking at each other could appear as two faces or look like a vase.

Similarly, *paradox illusions* offer pictures of things that simply cannot exist in real life. These illusions work because the brain expects to see certain shapes, and therefore fills in missing lines and shapes in an image because that is what the brain has learned to do over time. One example is in the famous optical

With cognitive optical illusions such as Rubin's vase (also known as Rubin face), the viewer's brain usually sees one of two valid interpretations and realizes there is a second image after some time or prompting.

illusion drawing of a staircase that appears to loop around without ever reaching any place. Finally, there are *distorting optical illusions,* where the information about length and distance, as related to the idea of perspective, are distorted. This happens when two parallel lines drawn in a specific way might appear to be approaching each other.

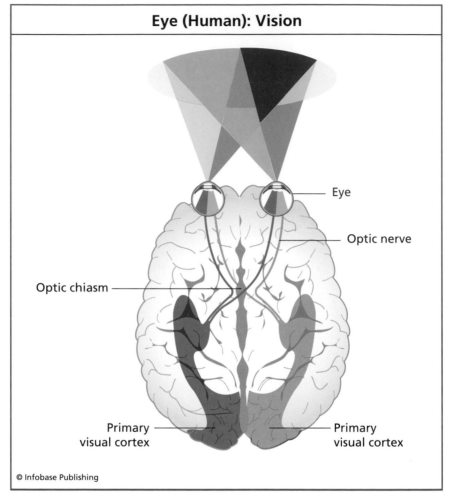

Eye (Human): Vision

Eye

Optic nerve

Optic chiasm

Primary
visual cortex

Primary
visual cortex

© Infobase Publishing

Vision is a complex process in which the eyes and the brain must
work together. Light first passes through the retina in the eye to
photoreceptor neurons, which pass signals to the brain. The brain
then processes this information and lets us know what we are seeing.

(continued from page 13)

not an illusion, as suggested in the theory of persistence of vision.
Rather, the brain-eye combination thinks that there is real movement going on. The alternative explanation remains somewhat
more complex than the persistence of vision theory. In general, the

persistence of vision theory remains the key way of explaining how motion is perceived.

No matter which theory explains the perception of motion, it is still true that specific still images need to be projected at a precise succession with dark spots between them for people to perceive the image as moving. In their simplest form, the still images could be hand drawn as stick figures with slight differences between each picture. When seen in close succession, the stick figures would appear to be moving. Cartoon movies do the same thing on a more sophisticated level. Artists produce each image, making one just a little bit different from the other in order to produce a sense of motion when the images are projected in the correct order. Movie cameras follow the same principle by capturing successive still images on film to produce multiple images that then are projected in a movie theater.

TRADITIONAL CINEMA

Even though Edison and the Lumière brothers were able to develop an early version of cinema, several challenges needed to be overcome in order for moving pictures to become popular. The technical challenge was finding the best way to capture the still images that would eventually produce the illusion of motion. This was tackled by the development of the camera and film that would be used to capture the images.

The problem of capturing images was solved by innovators who used the still camera and its film as a starting point. They developed a system in which the film would pass before the lens and stop for a moment. An image would be captured on the film, and then the next part of the film would come before the lens and stop, another image would be captured, and so on. This method produced a large length of film with individual images captured in the correct sequence and dark areas between each frame. Early movies were only able to capture about 16 or 20 frames in one second, creating the shaky and choppy images that were characteristic of the films of

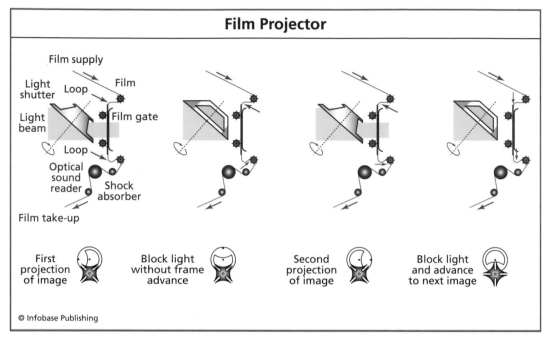

Film Projector

Film supply
Light shutter
Loop
Film
Light beam
Film gate
Loop
Optical sound reader
Shock absorber
Film take-up

First projection of image

Block light without frame advance

Second projection of image

Block light and advance to next image

© Infobase Publishing

Moving images are considered to be the product of an optical illusion in which single still images follow each other with moments of darkness. The film projector achieves this effect by systematically projecting successive images with intermittent dark stops by passing the film through a sophisticated gear and pulley system.

the 1920s. With developments in camera technology, it was possible to capture many more frames every second. This made the final moving picture appear smooth.

The photography process for movies required three different things to happen so that the illusion of movement could be produced for the audience: First, a section of the film had to be in front of the camera lens. Second, a section of the film would have to stay dark. Finally, another section of the film would have to take another photograph to show the new image in front of the camera. This whole process needed to happen about 24 times per second so that the motion would appear smooth and natural to viewers when they were shown each frame at a faster speed than which it was captured.

The instrument that would be able to do all the tasks required for the capture of motion was being developed at the same time by different inventors in Europe and the United States in the late 1800s: Thomas Edison in the United States, Edward Muybridge in England, and the Lumière brothers in France. They were all seeking a way to capture successive photographs of motion and to then show the photographs in a correct and rapid sequence to produce the illusion of motion. Muybridge actually set up a series of still cameras, each of which would take a photograph as a horse moved in front of it. Then the photographs would be shown in sequence to illustrate the motion of the horse.

Although inventors were able to produce the camera, the film, and the projection systems, there needed to be something to be captured and shown. At the time there was some degree of novelty to seeing motion on a screen, but that novelty was not enough to support an entire industry. Additionally, the technology was expensive and it was necessary to find a way to recover the cost of making a movie.

CAPTURING IMAGES AT A RAPID PACE

The problem of taking a series of pictures using a single camera device was partly solved when Hannibal Goodwin and George Eastman developed film that could be wrapped up in a roll. In addition, French inventor Louis Augustin Le Prince demonstrated that the little holes on the sides of film could be used to pull the film at a steady speed in front of the lens.

This resulted in the development of film industries in different parts of the world, with the pioneering work being done in the United States. Moving images became more than just a novelty. People would come to see those images because they narrated a comedy, a tragedy, a love story, or an action thriller. There was, therefore, a need for artists who could use the new technology to tell tales that would capture the imagination of people who would pay to watch movies just as they might go to the theater to see a play.

This led to the development of nickel theaters in U.S. cities, where people could go and watch a movie for one nickel. The first such theater opened in Philadelphia in 1905.

The development of the entertainment industry around the moving picture also motivated inventors to make improvements in the technology. The primary goal for the technological change was to make the experience of watching a film a more pleasing affair. Once it was clear that audiences were willing to pay five cents to watch a moving picture, it was also clear that the picture needed to look better. Choppy black and white movies that lasted for about 30 minutes would not be able to hold the interest that would be needed to feed an industry. It was also clear that if the technology could be improved and the content made more attractive, then the moving picture would offer a big business opportunity. This business opportunity was recognized by some of the pioneers of the entertainment industry in the United States, and led to changes in technology.

All of these late nineteenth-century and early twentieth-century developments, plus the realization that movies could be big business, led to ongoing developments in camera technology. The modern camera used for professional movie making has become an extremely complex and sophisticated tool, very efficient at capturing moving images. To get here, however, what was still needed in the early days was an efficient way of capturing the sound that accompanied the motion.

SYNCHRONIZING SOUND AND IMAGE

The early films that were shown in the nickel theaters of the United States only showed silent moving images. Often an orchestra would sit in a pit in front of the screen and play appropriate music to emphasize the mood of what was seen on screen. For example, a sad moment in the narrative would be accompanied by sad music, while action on screen would demand a different kind of music. There was no way of showing what the characters might

THE CLAPPERBOARD

One of the trickiest aspects of film-making has been the synchronization of movement and sound. There are several challenges to this process, two of which are critical. First, recording sound along with capturing visual images in real time is often a tricky process. The camera can capture the light and shade well, but the equipment required to make a crisp and clear sound recording is often more complicated. This is well illustrated in home movies made with amateur video cameras, in which the picture might look good but the sound of people speaking could be drowned out by noises in the environment. In professional filmmaking the sound is often recorded elsewhere and then added to the visual image. This requires the lip movements of the actors to be synchronized perfectly with the sound that is recorded and added later. The performers have to say all the words required of them in the script once on camera and then again in a recording room so that the image and sound can be synchronized.

The process of synchronization requires that a specific sound be *(continued)*

The clapperboard is used to synchronize picture and sound and identifies scenes and takes during a motion picture production.

(continued)

artificially created for what is happening on film. The camera needs to continuously record the following images once the first sound and image have been captured. If the recording must be stopped, a new sound cue must be used before another recording begins. These sound cues at the beginning of each recording segment offer the opportunity later to synchronize the sound and image. The most popular way of doing this is to use an instrument called the clapperboard. Every set of camera recordings must be started with a recording of the clapperboard.

In the early days of filmmaking the clapperboard consisted of two pieces of wood and a chalkboard. The scene number would be written on the chalkboard, and the two pieces of wood would be slammed together to produce the sound for future synchronization. Since then, the clapperboard has gone through many transformations and has today become digital. The digital clapperboard often does not even require that the sound be made with the clapperboard, because the digital board contains information called *time code,* which can be used to exactly match up the image and sound. The digital clapperboard, like the physical one of past years, still ensures that there is no mismatch between sound and image.

be saying on screen, nor the background sounds that would be heard in real life. The only way of showing dialogue was to insert occasional frames into the film with words quoting what the person was saying.

Sound recording requires that the sound waves had to be changed to electrical information that could later be translated back into sound through a set of instruments such as speakers. This difference meant that two kinds of instruments were needed to capture image and sound: One would capture the image, and the other would capture the accompanying sound. Capturing sound would require a microphone and the information would have to be recorded on a medium other than the film on which the image was recorded.

The difference in the recording process was further complicated by the fact that the sound had to match the image seen on the screen. For example, lip movements had to be precisely synchronized with the sound of the words being spoken. Even a slight lack of synchronization would appear awkward. One way of ensuring synchronization was to produce a properly synchronized sound and image that would be captured at the very beginning of a segment of film. The sound recording instrument would capture the sound, and the camera would capture the picture. Later these two would be synchronized to ensure that all the sound recorded was matched with the corresponding movements.

The year 1927 saw one of the first movies made with synchronized sound. *The Jazz Singer* was the first to not use an orchestra to play music, but instead the music was included with the film. This meant that viewers in every theater heard the same sound when watching the movie and were not dependent on what the orchestra played. The addition of dialogue also allowed for more complex stories to be told, since it was possible to keep viewers' attention with people speaking. These movies therefore needed less action. This was a great boon to the movie industry worldwide. It became clear that moving images would be a part of everyday life, so it was important to make improvements in order to increase the audience.

CAPTURING COLOR

The human eye is made up of different cells called rods and cones. These cells have evolved to recognize different shades of the three primary colors (red, green, and blue) and, through their combination, all the other colors are perceived. This process of perceiving colors happens when lights made up of the three different colors are mixed together to produce all the different hues that people are used to seeing. The image that is captured by a camera does the recording of color by combining lenses, and using special film that is able to retain a colored image. For moving pictures, each of the images is in color. When the light from the film projector passes through the colored film, it produces the colored image on the screen.

The key to producing colored images is the use of a special kind of film that is made up of three different chemical layers sensitive to the three primary colors. The color film captures an image through a process that creates a cloud of three colors on the film: yellow, magenta, and cyan. The various layers of the film are sensitive to different colored light and, when exposed, the different layers go through a chemical change. The resulting layers produce a film that retains an image, which acts as a color filter for light that passes through the film. For example, when a red glass is held up before a light source, only red light is seen through the glass. In a similar way, the film acts as a multi-colored filter, where the different hues are produced by the chemicals deposited on the film. When light from the projector passes through this film, the light gets filtered by the layers of chemicals. This produces the image that is seen on the screen.

The possibility of adding color to a moving image added to the quality of the image and therefore the way it could be used to tell a story. The film industry was able to recognize the value of this and quickly started to make films in color. Following the addition of sound and color, the moving image went through a series of other developments geared toward making the cinematic experience an increasingly exciting one.

IMPROVING THE MOVING IMAGE

By the middle of the 1930s, the basics of creating the moving image had been developed and movies were an established form of entertainment. This is the period when the film industry in the United States entered its golden age, built around studies such as Warner

Brothers and Metro-Goldwyn-Mayer. Movie stars such as Clark Gable and Greta Garbo emerged as well-known public figures.

The 1930s was also the time when another important technology was emerging. The moving image would no longer be captured on traditional film in the form of a chemical medium but would instead be captured as electrical signals that could be transmitted over the air. This was the beginning of the television industry, with many nations starting to experiment with the basics of television transmission. Most major cities had their own television stations. At this time, U.S. companies such as General Electric were also starting to manufacture television receivers that consumers could buy at a reasonable cost.

The emergence of television led to two significant changes in the technology of the production and distribution of the moving

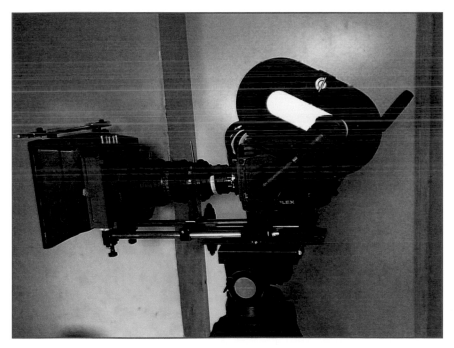

The movie camera is similar to a photographic camera in that it takes a rapid sequence of photos on strips of film. When the series of frames are played back quickly, usually at 24 frames per second, they create the illusion of motion.

image. First, the movie industry recognized that television could be a challenge for film, and thus film technology had to be improved in order to hold on to viewers. The improvements needed to demonstrate how film could be superior to television. This was achieved by changing the shape of the picture that was seen in the movie theaters. In the 1920s, a French professor named Henri Chrétien had developed a filming process called anamorphoscope, later purchased and renamed CinemaScope, in which a special lens combination could compress an image and place it on normal film. Later a similar arrangement of lenses could stretch the image, making it wider when it was shown in the theater. This resulted in a theatrical image that was more panoramic and not restricted to the boxier image that had been associated with cinema until that time.

This change in the shape of the image was particularly significant because the film technology with its lens combinations made it possible to produce larger images with greater detail. The anamorphic CinemaScope image was also followed by the 70 millimeter (mm) film image: The physical film was 70 mm (2.75 inches) in width, as compared to the traditional 35 mm films that were half that width. The doubling of the film size along with anamorphic filming allowed for the production of grand images, resulting in films like *Ben-Hur* (1959) and *The Sound of Music* (1965).

The second major change that occurred in moving image technology was improvement in the way sound was recorded for films. For most movies made before the 1960s, sound recording was done with a single microphone and all the sounds—the voices, the music, and the background sound—would appear to come from one source only. Humans are, however, able to detect the depth and direction of sound because we each have two ears. The sound recorded with a single microphone was unable to capture the richness of sound that one would experience in real life. In the 1930s, institutions such as Bell Laboratories in the United States developed the technology to capture sound with multiple microphones and play the sound back in a synchronized manner. The listener thus would be able to feel the direction from which the sound was coming. This was the beginning of further developments in the recording and playback of sound. Directionality was supplemented with depth, and listeners felt that they were surrounded by sound, creating a more realistic sound effect.

FILMING IN WIDESCREEN

The type of film that was used for traditional filmmaking was made up of a piece of celluloid that was 35 mm (1.37 inches) wide. This format allowed for the projection of an image whose ratio of height to width was 1.33, which made for a boxy image. The amount of detail that could be captured on the film was limited by the size of the film. The film industry decided that it was necessary to improve the quality of the image by altering its size so that the film audience would have a visual experience very different from television viewing.

The 70 mm film doubled the actual size of the film. This offered the opportunity to create more detailed images with more vibrant colors. The larger width of the film celluloid also offered the opportunity to place more detailed audio information on the film strip itself, allowing for a richer sound experience that was not possible on television. The wider film also changed the shape of the image, making it wider, with a new ratio of width to height of 2.20. The ratio, also called the aspect ratio, allowed for showing panoramic scenes packed with more details. This was a technology that was quite distinct from the anamorphic CinemaScope, where the size of the film did not change but optical methods were used to create the wide look. That method did not produce the more detailed image that the 70 mm film created.

The new format also spawned the possibility of producing extremely large images that could be projected on very big screens with special sound effects. One of the formats that became popular is IMAX. In IMAX films, the 70 mm film is used with a larger height, producing an image that is at least 72 feet wide and 52 feet tall (22 meters by 16 meters). The special cameras used for IMAX use the same film celluloid as the 70 mm film, but record the image so that a broader and taller picture is produced.

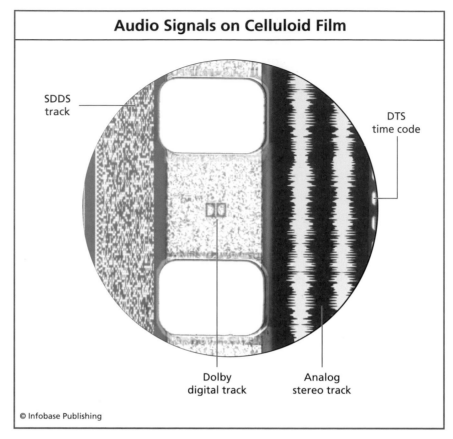

Audio Signals on Celluloid Film

SDDS track

DTS time code

Dolby digital track

Analog stereo track

© Infobase Publishing

The celluloid film used in film projectors not only contains the images that are projected on the screen, but also contains the audio information that is deciphered by the projector and sent to the sound system of a movie theater. The audio information is synchronized with the images and imprinted on one edge of the film.

The outcome of developments in image and sound technologies created a film industry that was able to capture the imagination of the audience. Realistic and convincing movies could be made with the new tools, showing the viewer panoramic vistas on the screen, accompanied with sound systems that could reconstruct the sounds of real life in the movie theater. Going to the movies became a pleasurable experience as theaters became more sophisticated with the implementation of better projectors, speakers, and seats for the audience.

The next significant change to image-capturing technology happened with the development of digital tools that could capture images and sounds by converting them to binary data instead of chemical and electrical information. Digital systems are made up of binary data, with all information being recorded as a combination of the digits 0 and 1.

How to Make Digital Video

Capturing moving images on film is an expensive task. It requires a sophisticated camera that must accomplish several different operations such as transporting the film at a steady rate and capturing numerous still images in a precise manner. In the past, most of the cameras used for this process were meant to be run by professional operators making movies or television shows. This process changed with the development of electronic technologies. The process of capturing images then moved away from the film to the electronic media.

This move was made possible with the development of technology that allowed an image captured by a lens to be converted to electrical information that could be stored on magnetic tape. The process was developed in the late 1920s by scientists Philo Farnsworth and Vladimir Zworykin, who developed systems that used the combination of a lens and light-sensitive material to develop basic image capture devices. All the devices depended on the fact that some metals emit electrons when exposed to light. These are called photosensitive metals. They can be exposed to different levels of light, and the level of exposure can be recorded as an electrical voltage. This eliminated the need for film since there was no reason to store the image. It was only necessary to record the electrical information, which could be stored on magnetic tape in the same way that sound is recorded as electrical information on cassettes.

The video camera operates as an instrument that is able to convert light and shade into electrical information that can be stored. The quality of the image depends on the type of lens used to capture

Unlike movie cameras, which record images on film, video cameras create electronic moving images. In the beginning, video cameras were very large machines that came in two sections. Originally used mainly in television studios, video cameras today have numerous uses and designs, including film production, surveillance and monitoring purposes, and scientific research.

the image and the device used to convert the image into electrical signals. Just like the traditional film camera, the video camera also has to capture a set number of still images every second, which are shown in quick succession to produce the illusion of motion. In the case of the video camera, however, the images are captured as successive frames by storing the electrical information about each frame. It is important that the electrical information accurately represents the original images captured by the lens.

A key development that led to greater precision in the conversion of light and shade into electrical information was the charge-coupled device (CCD). This device could be used to precisely record the electrical signal related to the light falling on a photosensitive material. The CCD was invented in the 1950s by two scientists at Bell Laboratories, Willard Boyle and George Smith. The CCD was a smaller device than the ones used in some of the earlier methods of converting light and shade into electrical information and was soon adopted with most video cameras. The CCD made it possible to easily convert an image into electrical information that could be stored as variations in voltage on a magnetic tape. The information about the image remained as analog data based on the variations in voltage.

The next significant change happened when it became possible to convert analog voltage information into binary numbers through a process of digitization. The voltage recorded by each portion of the CCD would be converted to a number made up of the digits 0 and 1. This was accomplished by the analog to digital converter (ADC), which would convert a specific voltage value into a binary number. Once the CCD was divided into tiny portions, an image could be recorded as a series of binary numbers, each representing the amount of light falling on a specific portion of the CCD. All the numbers together would make up the image.

A digital video camera is based on the principle of digitization. The camera is made up of three specific parts. First, the digital camera uses a sophisticated lens to capture the image. This is not very different from traditional film cameras, whose lens quality determined the quality of the image captured on film. Most digital

The charge-coupled device (CCD) is a light-sensitive circuit that stores and displays data for an image. Each pixel in the image is converted into an electrical charge in which the intensity is related to a color in the color spectrum. CCDs are used in a variety of devices, including digital still and video cameras, telescopes, scanners, and bar code readers.

video cameras use the same kind of lens used in traditional cameras. A good lens ensures that an appropriate amount of light is allowed to enter the camera.

The second part of the digital video camera is the CCD or similar device that converts the image into electrical information. The quality of the CCD is determined by the size of the device. Larger CCDs that are about one half of an inch (1.25 centimeters) in size are considered to be the higher quality CCDs. The size of the CCD determines the amount of light that it can capture. The CCD is also broken down into tiny segments, each of which is called a pixel. Light falling on each pixel is converted to a binary number; therefore, larger amounts of pixels allow for greater detail to be captured.

Finally, video cameras need to have an efficient way of storing the binary information that is captured by the CCD. The most common storage device in most digital video cameras used to be magnetic tape. This tape is similar to audio cassettes, but the tape is able to store a binary data file. Some cameras use a compact disc (CD) or digital video disc (DVD) to store the information as well, and many use a digital memory card that operates like a small computer hard drive. There has been some criticism about the use of discs to store digital images, since these cameras take longer to start up than tape-based cameras. At the same time, disc-based cameras produce a DVD that can be used with standard DVD players. Tape-based cameras require special cables to connect the camera to a TV to watch the pictures.

Digital video is stored as a series of binary numbers that produce different kinds of digital files. The ADC is able to produce different kinds of digital files with different levels of detail about the original image. Files that hold on to all details using a large CCD with many pixels are often extremely large in size; it is possible, however, to produce smaller files that do not contain as much detail.

Users have the option to select the kind of file in which they want to store their information. Most personal computers are able to interpret the different file formats and display the image. The images in files that store fewer details do not look as good as the images produced from larger, more detailed files. The fact that the image is nothing other than a digital file also makes it possible to produce similar files without using a computer.

CREATING DIGITAL VIDEO

The most common form of storing digital video is a standardized format approved by the Motion Picture Experts Group (MPEG), called MPEG-4. This format was developed in 1998. It uses a mathematical process to create a binary file that stores both the audio and image information in a way that can be interpreted by most computers. A computer can display motion as long as there is a digital file that contains the information about the images.

It is not always necessary to use a camera to capture motion; it is possible for computer programmers to create a moving image by writing a digital file using a computer alone. This process begins with the development of a series of computer-generated images that show imaginary objects that appear to be moving. The most common way of doing this is to start with a simple image of an object and then show successive images of tiny segments of motion. For example, it is possible to create a stick figure on the computer and then write a program that moves the stick figure by tiny amounts. When the images are displayed rapidly on a computer screen, the viewer witnesses an illusion of motion. Later, it is possible to enhance the stick figure with details to make it look real—like an animal or a human being, for example.

No camera ever plays a role in this process. The entire image is created using computer programs, but the final moving image could appear quite realistic. This is a method that is often used to make animated films, as in the case of the 2007 movie *Ratatouille*. Pixar Studios created this film entirely with spectacular computer-generated images. Such movies have become possible with the development of complex computer systems that allow artists to work with computer programs to create digital images that do not exist in real life.

Some digital video combines real video images with images created by computers. In this case, a camera is used to capture moving images that are then used as the starting point for creating digital files. This process allows artists to merge the real images with computer-generated ones. This is used when it is important to show realistic subtleties in the movements and expressions of a digital character. For example, this process was used in the 2006 film *Pirates of the Caribbean: Dead Man's Chest*. The role of the imaginary character Davy Jones was played by a real actor whose movements and expressions were digitally captured with a digital camera. Those

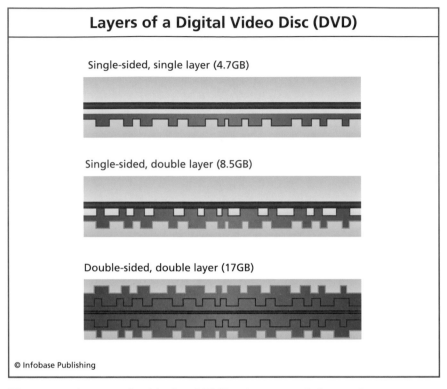

Layers of a Digital Video Disc (DVD)

Single-sided, single layer (4.7GB)

Single-sided, double layer (8.5GB)

Double-sided, double layer (17GB)

© Infobase Publishing

There are three major kinds of DVDs that store information on different layers that are read off by the laser. A larger amount of information can be stored on discs that have a larger number of layers. Most commercial DVD movies are distributed on double-sided, double-layered discs.

expressions were later merged with the face of the digital Davy Jones, which was created completely with computer programs. The resulting image showed the expressions of the human actor on the digital, tentacle-covered face of Davy Jones.

Digital video can also be created from analog sources whose original information is converted to a digital file. This is often used to create digital versions of moving images that were captured and stored on film or videotape. Digital cameras for commercial media use have only become popular since the late 1990s. Before that, almost all moving images were captured on film or videotape. People these days are converting their older material to digital files before the film or videotape begins to decay with age. Digital files can be stored on a DVD, which is expected to last longer than film or videotape.

There are special tools that can be used to convert film to digital files. The process became popular in the late 1990s when special equipment became available to do this conversion. In 1997 Robert Michael, the information technology editor of the *Library Journal*, reported on equipment developed by Fuji Film Corporation that could convert 16 mm film into digital files. Since such equipment is quite expensive, many companies offer a conversion service. Customers can simply send in their film and get a digital file in return.

Digital moving images also play a role in many different kinds of digital documents. This is most popular with Web sites that include some form of moving image that is not necessarily captured with a camera. Computer programmers are able to use software like Flash to create simple moving images that can be easily incorporated into other computer programs. It has become increasingly easy to create simple digital animations for a variety of applications, including Internet-based tools, computer games, and full-length feature films. The primary concern with all digital video is the large size of the binary files that require efficient means of storage and manipulation.

HANDLING DIGITAL FILES

Digital video is made up of single frames of still pictures that are used to create the illusion of motion. Each individual image is made up of binary numbers that represent the amount of light falling on a specific pixel of the CCD. At 24 frames per second, there are 24 still images for every second in a digital video. A one-minute video would be made up of 1,440 still images, which need to be displayed at exactly 24 frames per second to produce the moving image. If fewer frames are displayed, the motion would appear choppy and unrealistic, while a quicker display of frames would make the image appear to be moving too fast.

FLASH AS A TOOL FOR IMAGES

Web site creators regularly use video and animation to embellish the look of their sites. The moving images on Web sites need to be made up of small files that can be interpreted by any computer so that a user can easily view them. Some of those images could be animations generated by the computer, while others could be images captured with a camera and then converted to a format that can be easily included on a Web site.

One format that has been popular is called Flash Video, which was first developed by Jonathan Gay in 1993 through a company called FutureWave Software. The Flash program initially used stick figures produced with a computer program to create simple animations. The program was taken over by the Macromedia Corporation in 1996 and emerged as a popular way of developing video files for distribution over the Internet. It was eventually taken over again, this time by the Adobe Corporation, which provides many different computer programs for manipulating images and video. The main advantage of the Flash program is that programmers can use it along with standard ways of creating Web sites so that the video blends seamlessly with a site.

The quality of the image depends on how much detail is captured in every still image. Professional video cameras with larger CCDs, as discussed earlier, can hold thousands of pixels. That information needs to be instantly recorded on a tape or DVD to ensure that all the information of each still image is held in memory. The process of converting the information of an image and into a digital file eventually produces extremely large files that are difficult to store and manipulate.

A digital video file can be so large that it requires special storage systems such as DVDs to capture the entire file. Sometimes the material being stored is so large that one DVD cannot hold all the information. For example, the 1960s movie *The Sound of Music* is nearly three hours long and requires two DVDs to store its digital version. A digital video camera that uses DVDs to store the captured moving images usually cannot store more than 60 minutes of video on each disc. Users therefore have to change discs as they capture more video.

In 1980, computer scientists such as Leonardo Chiariglione and his colleagues at Telecom Italia's CSELT research center began developing specific methods of managing digital video file size. The most common way of managing a video file is by artificially reducing the size of the file using a process called compression. A compressed file becomes smaller in size because the computer can apply a mathematical formula to recreate a digital image instead of storing every detail of the image.

For example, in a video of a family vacation showing people on a beach with a clear blue sky, there is no need to record the information about the color of the sky for each of the 24 frames captured for each second of video. Instead, that information is stored for a few frames. When the image is later displayed, the computer can recreate the blue sky. The resulting digital file is now smaller in size, but part of the accuracy of the image might be diminished because some of the subtle variations could be lost through the process of compression. Similar loss in quality also occurs when the size of a file is reduced by decreasing the number of pixels used to create the image. It is possible to use fewer pixels to capture an image, and each pixel would have fewer details about the image. This produces a smaller file that might not look very good when displayed.

A key issue with the size of digital video files is determining the kind of display device to be used to see the moving images. As a general rule, files of lower quality look inferior when shown on a large screen. Therefore, it is best to display low-quality files on smaller screens such as a 12-inch (30-cm) computer monitor, rather than a 20-inch (50-cm) monitor. The decision about the size of the final file is often based on the quality of the display device to be used, as well as the function of the file.

The size of the file also has an impact on the way the file can be distributed. Larger files require larger storage systems, such as portable hard drives or DVDs. Smaller files can be stored on other memory devices that are smaller in size. Smaller files can also be easily shared among networked computers, or computers that are hooked up to each other. Since the digital video file is

IMAGE SIZE

The large number of devices that can use digital video files has led to the development of numerous compression methods that produce the ideal image for a specific device. Digital video files can be blown up to produce an image that is usually seen in a movie theater, or can be shrunk to fit on the tiny display screen of a cell phone. These different versions of images could start with the same original digital file that might have been captured with the highest possible detail using a professional digital video camera. Later, that image is compressed into different formats for use with different devices. Although it is possible to reduce the size of the digital file and create images with fewer details, it is impossible to increase the details of a digital file once it

has been captured. Users need to be careful that the video is captured in a manner that would produce a clear image even when displayed on a large device.

The fact that digital video can be resized into many dimensions has made it possible to include moving images into many kinds of digital devices. You no longer need to have access to a computer to watch digital video. If the file is available in the appropriate format, it can be viewed on a television screen, the display screen of a cell phone, or on small screens that are popular in many cars. The smaller-sized images are also able to be quickly distributed to a large number of people. Since cell phones are always connected to a cell phone network, it is possible to easily send video files from one cell no different from any other digital files, the video file can easily be sent from one computer to another using networks such as the Internet. The main barrier to sending large files is the size of the file, since smaller files take up fewer network resources. Files that are intended to be shared over the Internet arc expected to be smaller in size and are not usually expected to have as much

DVD players are now portable and are used in a variety of locations, including homes, offices, and even cars.

phone to another. This capability of sharing smaller images with fewer dotails has helped develop special connections among people, who can now share a video image of an experience with each other.

clarity as digital files that are distributed on DVDs and other memory devices.

The size of a digital file is something that the user controls. He or she can decide the specific size that is desirable based on how the digital video file will be used. At the same time, the user has to be careful about the compatibility of the digital file. Different kinds of compression techniques produce different kinds of digital files, each of which require appropriate computer programs to decipher the file and display it. For example, a digital file that was produced with Apple's QuickTime compression might not work well with a computer that uses the Windows system. Incompatibilities like that have led to the development of some compression techniques that produce files that can be interpreted by most computers. Among these formats, the mp4 format (official name is MPEG-4 Part 14, which was discussed earlier) has become the most popular. Most computers are able to interpret the mp4 format to produce the image. The method of compression producing the mp4 format also produces a file that retains a large amount of detail, making the image look good. The files are also small enough that it is possible to send them over networks, even though it could take up to several hours to download a complete movie that uses the mp4 format.

Another format that is popular for use with the Internet is the Windows Media Video (WMV) format, developed by the Microsoft Corporation. This format produces smaller files that can be easily sent over the Internet. With the growing availability of connections to the Internet that allow rapid flow of data, this format can be used to display video on Web sites. Many Web sites include video along with pictures, sound, and text. The WMV format allows a user to watch video on his or her computer without downloading the digital file to the computer. The data is sent in a continuous stream. Because of the smaller file size, computers are able to rapidly interpret the data and display it on the screen.

Displaying Digital Images

Data suggests that digital video is becoming more popular among those interested in capturing moving images. For example, in 2005 a popular drugstore chain in the United States began selling a disposable video camera for under $30. An analyst who works with the camera industry claimed that nearly 40 percent of all images would be captured using cameras that are disposed after a single use. The devices that display images are therefore an important tool.

As explained earlier, the process of digitizing moving images begins with converting the electrical information captured by the CCD into a number that can be stored using the binary system. Each pixel of the CCD generates a number, all of which together contain the information about the image. These numbers have to be converted back into electrical signals that can be used to create an image that will be identical to the one captured by the

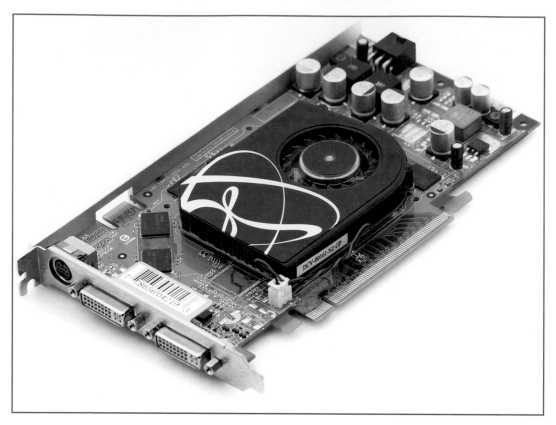

A video card, also called a graphics card, receives binary information about an image from the computer's microprocessor (or CPU) and decides how to use that data to create the image. This information is then sent to the computer monitor through a cable and translated into the millions of pixels that make the picture.

CCD. The first part of the reconversion is done by a computer program that can interpret the information stored in the digital video file.

For example, the Windows Media Player program, which is included with all computers using the Windows system, is able to interpret digital video files that use the MPEG-4 format or the WMV format. This computer program reads the numbers in the digital file and sends corresponding information to the digital to analog converter (DAC), which is required to connect a computer monitor to a computer. The DAC is often called the "video card" of a computer. It takes the information from programs like Windows Media Player and converts the digital information into analog electrical signals that can be sent to the computer monitor to display the picture.

Once again, the quality of the final picture is dependent on the amount of information contained in the digital file that is used to store the image information. A highly compressed file will contain less information, making it impossible to obtain an image of very high quality. The ability to watch a moving image is then dependent on the computer program used to interpret the file, because the digital file has to be compatible with the program being used. If the program cannot process the digital file, no image will appear on the screen.

The image is also dependent on the video card used to convert the digital information into electrical signals. This process has to happen at a quick pace, in which 24 frames can be displayed on the monitor per second. The quality of the picture depends on the speed at which the video card can process the data and display it on the monitor. With digital video files becoming commonplace in many digital applications, video cards have become an important piece of technology.

THE MONITOR

A computer monitor reverses the task of a camera by converting the electrical signals from the video card into light and shade. These areas of light and shade combine to reproduce the image that was originally captured by the camera. Just like the camera captured 24 frames every second, the monitor displays the frames in quick succession, creating the illusion of motion. The picture seen on the computer monitor is made up of pixels similar to the ones in the CCD that was used to capture the image. The monitor screen is divided into tiny pixels, with each pixel receiving a specific instruction from the video card to display a certain intensity and color. For example, if a pixel on the CCD captured the color red, the equivalent pixel of the screen would display the same red. In this manner, the image is rebuilt, pixel by pixel.

The quality of the image is dependent on the number of pixels that can be handled by a display. Images with fewer pixels create grainy pictures with less detail. "The display adapter and monitor you use can make a big difference in your computing enjoyment," notes an article in the *PC Magazine Encyclopedia*. Since many users spend a significant amount of time before a monitor, it is important to use a good display device for more enjoyment.

FROM CRT TO LCD

The kind of computer monitor that was used in the early days of computing was very similar to a traditional television set. It was made up of a cathode ray tube (CRT), a large piece of equipment that needed a fair amount of desk space and was relatively heavy. Most desktop computers of the 1980s required a CRT, making it difficult to move the computer from one place to another since the monitor could weigh up to 50 pounds (23 kilograms). The CRT monitor produces a very sharp and bright picture but is limited in size. The largest monitor is about 17 inches (43 cm) in length when measured diagonally from the top left-hand corner to the bottom right-hand corner. Although the CRT remained a popular type of computer display until 2004 or 2005, it was quickly replaced by the liquid crystal display (LCD). This new kind of monitor was popularized by laptop computers, which could not use a CRT.

The LCD became popular in the 1970s when it was used as the display device for digital watches that only required a display with two colors: black and white. That kind of a display was adopted for the laptop computers of the late 1980s, when there was a demand for a portable, lightweight computer. The LCD provided a solution for the weight problem associated with the CRT, but the LCD did not provide a picture that was as bright as the CRT monitor. This drawback was resolved in 2000, when LCD

One key issue about a computer monitor is its multi-purpose use. A computer monitor is used for everyday computing activities such as writing papers or doing financial calculations, but also for looking at digital pictures and watching videos. It is important that the same monitor be able to perform the different tasks equally well. A low-quality monitor would not be able to display high-quality images, but it could be quite sufficient for other purposes.

The monitor also plays an important role in decisions on how the original digital video image is produced. Images that are supposed

technology improved enough to produce very bright and extremely light monitors that could be used for any kind of computer.

By 2004, sales of the LCD monitor exceeded those of the CRT monitor. LCD technology was also adopted by the television industry as most television sets evolved into digital devices. This made the LCD a better option than the CRT. The LCD is a truly digital device because it creates a picture by recreating the specific pixels that make up the picture. An LCD screen is a combination of rows and columns of pixels that are illuminated to show an exact replica of the original digital image.

The success of the LCD was also driven by widespread consumer preference of this technology because the LCD monitor became affordable for most users. Writing a review of LCD monitors in 2003, Alfred Poor of *PC Magazine* stated that their lowered price was driven by the "drop in manufacturing costs for LCD panels, which are the most expensive components in LCD monitors." The less expensive LCD offered an excellent picture that could be displayed on a large-screened monitor that didn't take up too much space. Since the LCD monitor is relatively thin, it is possible to hang it on a wall or build it into a flat surface. The LCD's benefits are so vast, in fact, that Sony Corporation, a major manufacturer of CRT displays, decided in 2007 to completely focus on the LCD for future products. It is likely that the flat-panel LCD will emerge as the most popular display device of the future.

to be shown on large monitors need to be captured with a great deal of detail, and the image must remain relatively uncompressed so that all its details are clear. Other images that are meant for small monitors, or are sent over the Internet to be watched in a small window on a computer screen, do not need to have a great amount of detail. The need for a match between the way the video is produced and the monitor used to watch it is especially important, because if the matching is done incorrectly, the image will appear quite poor. For example, if a video on a Web site is sent to a large monitor, the image would appear very hazy since it was built with just a limited number of pixels.

It is important to pay attention to the way an image is captured to ensure it matches the specifications of the monitor on which the image will eventually be displayed. It is possible to reduce the size of a picture from one with a lot of detail to one that has fewer details and is suitable for smaller displays. This is often done when the same video image is compressed in different ways to suit different displays, as is the case of some television shows. The original video image of the show might be compressed to a format and size that is suitable for Web-based distribution. The fact that the image starts as a digital file gives it the flexibility to alter it in any way to fit different needs.

RANGE OF VIEWING DEVICES

The quality of digital video is closely related to the kind of viewing device that is selected to watch the video. The quality of the video is highest when the video format and the viewing device match each other. Some viewing devices are used by individuals who are sitting down to watch videos. A computer monitor—desktop or laptop—falls into this category because the computer user usually has to be sitting in front of a monitor to watch a video.

Most of these monitors are either cathode ray tube (CRT) or liquid crystal display (LCD) devices. Some computer monitors might also have a plasma display, but these are usually meant to

HEAD MOUNTED DISPLAYS

The head mounted display (HMD) is an example of a wearable computer. The user wears a special gadget that allows interaction with the computer in a very realistic way. The HMD works like a pair of eyeglasses, where the lenses are replaced with some form of an LCD screen and lens combination. This cuts off the user from the outside world and allows him or her to be immersed in whatever is being displayed on the HMD.

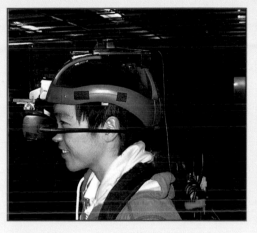

Head mounted displays are used for tactical purposes by the military and fire and police departments; for medical and technical procedures by engineers and scientists; and for entertainment applications

Some HMDs also offer a see-through option. The user can see everything happening around him or her, and the HMD adds additional information to this image. The see-through HMD is often used by military personnel such as fighter pilots, who need to see what is around and also constantly check the status of certain parts of the plane. A similar device is a simpler version of the HMD, where a soldier can flip down an eyepiece connected to the helmet and see the location of other soldiers, information about the enemy, and other important information. Noah Shachtman of *Popular Mechanics* pointed out the value of these units in a 2007 article: "Instead of relying on the hand signals and shouted orders that most infantrymen use, Alpha company [a military unit] communicates via advanced, encrypted radio transmissions." Such transmissions end up as digital data that is displayed through a helmet-mounted digital eyepiece.

Civilians also use HMD as a key tool for virtual games meant to

(continues)

(continued)

immerse the player in a computer-generated playing space. Commercially produced HMDs also allow users to watch their favorite videos and television shows privately in places where it might be difficult to see a large screen image. For example, one such product is the iTheater, highlighted by *Coolest Gadgets* magazine in 2006. This device "is a personal entertainment center that you wear as if they were glasses," according to the magazine.

These products are an extension of the idea of headphones, which allow a user to be cut off from the sounds of the world while enjoying music from a personal music player. The HMD does the same thing with vision, immersing the user in an environment that is totally cut off from the real world. The most important benefit of HMDs is the sense of immersion that they produce. Researchers Doug Bowman and Ryan McMahan of Virginia Tech reported in 2007 that "the goal of immersive virtual environments (VEs) was to let the user experience a computer-generated world as if it were real—producing a sense of presence, or 'being there,' in the user's mind."

be used indoors when connected to a computer's video card. Some portable computers are manufactured in such a way that the screen can also be viewed in bright light. Most such devices must also be connected to a computer. They do not operate as standalone viewing devices because the information used to create the picture on the screen must arrive from the video card of the computer. These devices are also usually meant for personal use because it could be very inconvenient for many people to huddle around a computer screen to watch a video.

The main disadvantage of the traditional computer monitor described here is that these devices are not very useful if a person is traveling. For example, it is dangerous to watch a video screen while driving a car. At the same time, there is a need for display devices that are portable and affordable. People cannot always be in front of a computer monitor but might still need access to digital video.

This need is fulfilled by putting display devices on gadgets such as the cell phone, personal digital assistant (PDA), and personal media viewing gadgets like Apple's iPod and iPhone. These gadgets use very small display devices, often made up of tiny LCD screens that can show video. The screens may be very bright and are usually able to show a fairly sharp picture. These devices are becoming increasingly popular. Along with their popularity, there is a growing amount of video content being prepared for viewing on smaller

Due to advanced technology, viewers can store and play digital media anywhere and at any time. Portable media players (PMPs) like this one are capable of playing audio and video and storing images. The Apple iPod Touch, one of the most popular PMPs, received Editor's Choice awards from some of the top digital technology magazines in the country, including CNET, *PC Magazine*, and *Laptop Magazine*.

screens. For example, many production companies in the United States make some of their popular television programs available for download from their company Web sites. People who have tools such as the iPod can download these special video files and watch them on a media player's small screen.

The cell phone is also becoming a tool whose small LCD display can be used to display video. The cell phone has the added advantage of having a network connection, so video files can be continuously sent from user to user. A digital file is sent wirelessly to a cell phone just like any other digital files. People with video cell phones can watch video on them as if they were watching a television program on TV. South Korea and Japan have been leaders in the use of the cell phone for receiving television programs.

The ability to receive digital video files on the small screens of cell phones and portable media players offers the user the opportunity to watch video at any time. These images are of inferior quality, however, and they cannot reproduce the richness of the images seen on a television screen or in a movie theater. This has led to the development of a class of display devices that are designed to project a large image from a digital file and mimic the experience of sitting in a movie theater. This trend has created a new demand for home theaters, where people can convert an entire room into a small movie theater by installing the appropriate video and audio tools.

The home theater has become possible because of the development of LCD technology, which has been adopted by the television industry. LCD technology has led to the manufacture of flatscreen televisions that can produce a very bright and large picture. In 2006, the Japanese company Sharp Electronics demonstrated the largest LCD television set at the annual Consumer Electronics Show. The television produced a picture that was 82 inches (208 cm) in size when measured diagonally from its top left-hand corner to its bottom right-hand corner. The following year Sharp topped itself by introducing the 108-inch (274-cm) Aquos LCD television.

LCD televisions are the most widely produced and sold today. They are much lighter because they do not use heavy glass faces, are much thinner, and can be built at any size.

Such large pictures make it possible to set up in one's home a room with a large LCD display and comfortable seating, just like a movie theater. These devices can be connected with good audio and video tools such as DVD players and surround sound systems to further the theater effect. The home theater provides a way of enjoying a movie without having to go out to a commercial theater. As journalist Katie Hafner pointed out in the *New York Times* in 2002, it's like watching "a film from within the confines of your own domestic fortress."

The popularity of this concept has led to the increased production of gadgets that make it easy to set up a home theater. Many consumers have opted to buy LCD projectors that project pictures as large as 120 inches (305 cm) across onto a white wall, creating even more of a movie theater effect. Homes are being designed to have a space dedicated for a home theater, where the display device not only acts as a screen for watching television programs and movies, but can also be connected to digital game systems and computers.

Digital Video
and Mass Media

The quality of a digital image on a display screen is related to the number of pixels that are shown on the screen. The best image that can currently be produced has 1,920 columns and 1,200 rows of pixels. This adds up to more than 2 million pixels, offering a great deal of detail to the image. An image with that level of detail is called a high-definition (HD) picture. This is increasingly becoming the desired level of detail for most video images. Based on instructions from the Federal Communications Commission (FCC) in the United States, all television broadcasts in the country were converted to digital HD by the spring of 2009.

The main reason the FCC pushed for the transition of all U.S. television broadcasts to digital HD was to improve the quality of television services in the country. The adoption of the digital HD standard requires television broadcasters to use special electromagnetic waves to transmit information. This frees up the existing parts of the electromagnetic spectrum for use in other crucial activities

Although most motion pictures are shot on film, directors have begun to use high-definition digital video cameras. Most of these cameras are used for films with special effects due to the ease of transfer to digital editing systems and the high quality of HD video. Shooting in HD also allows filmmakers, especially those without studio support, to be able to afford longer shoots because there is no more expensive film stock and costly telecine equipment (used to transfer film into video), and scenes can be played back as soon as they have been shot.

related to national security. The viewer also benefits from a better television viewing experience with clearer pictures, greater choice of programs on cable television, and the ability to personalize programming received at home.

The first digital HD television (HDTV) was developed in Japan in 1968. Commercial HDTV became available to Japanese viewers in the 1980s. There was not enough interest in HDTV in the United States until the late 1990s. The U.S. media industry then became more attentive to this technology, eventually leading to the FCC ruling that was signed into law by President George W. Bush in 2006. The transition required that both the producers of television programs and the viewer obtain new digital tools to create and receive HDTV broadcasts.

At the beginning of the transition, the HD image was made up of 1,280 columns and 720 rows of pixels. This changed the shape of the picture on the screen. The traditional picture had a 4 to 3 ratio of length to height. The new picture had a more panoramic look with a length-to-height ratio of 16 to 9. The change in the ratio made the picture appear more attractive. Also, with nearly one million pixels, it contained a significant amount of detail.

The way the picture is produced on the screen also changes with HDTV. The picture on the screen is usually produced by illuminating every row of pixels at a rapid rate to create the illusion of motion. In traditional television the screen was illuminated starting at the top left-hand corner, with the first line on the screen being lit up. The next line to be lit up was the third line, then the fifth, and so on until the bottom of the screen was reached. The process would then start at the second line of the screen and proceed to the bottom lighting up the even-numbered lines. The process happened at a very rapid pace and the viewer would not notice that alternating lines were being drawn to create the picture. This process is called interlaced drawing of an image.

Although the eye does not perceive the alternating lines, a better picture is produced if consecutive lines are progressively lit up. Standard HDTV uses this progressive method. This is why HDTV is sometimes referred to as 720p television, to indicate the number of rows and the way they are illuminated. The progressive method produces a sharp and detailed image.

The quality of HDTV is also closely related to the way the image is produced. As pointed out earlier, the look of the digital image is dependent on a match between the instrument used to capture the moving image and the display used to view it. The transition to HDTV required television stations in the United States to install new digital tools to ensure that a 720p picture could be transmitted. The new equipment was able to produce shows that had the high quality that is expected of HDTV. Older shows or movies shown on television that had been captured with older equipment don't necessarily look much better just because the broadcast is done digitally.

There must also be changes at the receiving end of the signal. Older TV sets cannot operate with the digital transmission, and

HDTV

The decision by the FCC to order the complete conversion of all U.S. television broadcasts to the HDTV standard is supposed to be followed by such an adoption at the worldwide level. The shift from traditional broadcast television to the HDTV standard is one of the most significant changes in television technology since television became a global medium in 1950. The motivation to change to HDTV came mainly from the television industry, which recognized that HDTV would allow companies to sell a large set of services to viewers and could generate more interest in watching television.

The success of HDTV is closely related to the way the HD image is created. The entire image is made up of numerous pixels that are illuminated by an electrical signal. Each pixel illuminates itself based on the instruction provided by the video card or an equivalent piece of equipment. Like all digital video, the quality of the image is dependent on the number of pixels used to create it. Along with the pixels, the HD image creates an illusion of motion by rapidly displaying a series of still images that are just a bit different from each other. Successively viewing the images creates the sense of motion that the viewer sees.

There are two ways an HD still image is generated: either by illuminating pixels on alternate rows of the screen or illuminating pixels on consecutive rows. The latter produces a sharper picture and is called progressive scanning. Since these two factors have the most impact on the quality of the consumers require appropriate television sets or suitable accessories in order to receive the digital broadcast signal and interpret the digital information to produce an image. Many older television sets are obsolete in the age of HDTV. This has led to some confusion among customers, who are troubled by the fact that their trusted television sets need additional equipment to operate with HDTV.

picture, all HD images are described in terms of the number of rows used to create the image and the way the pixels are illuminated. In 2008, the best picture quality was obtained by using 1,080 rows of pixels that are illuminated progressively. This is why the best HDTV monitor is usually called a 1080p monitor. All other monitors are somewhat inferior to the 1080p, and only experimental monitors can display a picture at a higher definition. A new system that will have 7,680 columns and 4,320 rows of pixels is being developed through a partnership between private industry and the Japanese government.

The success of HDTV is also related to the instrument used to create the HD content. To achieve the best results, the camera used to create HD pictures must also operate at 1080p and capture the highest quality picture available. Most of the content used in HDTV broadcasts happens at 720p, which means that a 1080p monitor would not be used to its highest capacity.

The HDTV broadcast method is also a significant change from the traditional mode of sending television signals. The HDTV broadcast uses binary data to send the image information, and an ordinary television with traditional television antennas is not able to receive the broadcast. The television set needs a special kind of antenna that will be able to decipher the HDTV broadcast, and then needs a special computer processor able to decipher the digital message. These requirements suggest that the viewer will have to change the television set, or add accessories to make it possible to enjoy the HDTV broadcast.

For example, "[c]able customer Doris Spurk was surprised to learn that thanks to the transition, she would have to rent a converter box for $5.95 per month, per television set, plus pay for a $60 service call to install it," wrote a *USA Today* reporter in 2008. "With five televisions in her home, the conversion would increase her bill by 75%." These problems will eventually be resolved as HDTV becomes the standard mode of transmitting television signals and people recognize the benefit of the better picture and the interactivity that digital technology offers.

Since the video image that is received arrives as a binary data file, HDTV offers opportunities of interacting with the image in ways that were impossible with traditional television. In the case of HDTV, the digital file can be stored on computer memory in the television set. Later on, the stored file can be manipulated in different ways. For example, HDTV offers the opportunity to set a live broadcast on pause. If someone is watching a basketball game on television and wants to get up for a drink of water, he or she can set the television picture on pause and begin watching again from the stopping point. The digital file is held in temporary storage while the viewer has set the picture on pause, and the stored file is played back when the viewer starts to watch again. Thereafter, the viewer will lag slightly behind the live action, but without missing a moment of it.

Enhanced user control is possible simply because all the information is being sent as binary data that can be altered with appropriate computer technology. The sender can also make changes to the image by manipulating the digital file that is broadcast. One simple method of controlling the broadcast is by putting a small delay between the time when the image is captured and when the image is broadcast. This allows the sender to ensure that no questionable material is being broadcast. The use of HDTV also allows the broadcaster to be able to do special effects such as action replays when broadcasting sports programs.

The use of digital HDTV offers new opportunities to broadcasters to create new kinds of content for the viewer. The content not only looks good but changes the viewing experience by allowing the user a great deal of interactivity and management of what is being viewed. This is possible because the entire broadcast is made up of digital files that can be manipulated by both the sender and the receiver.

COMPLETE DIGITAL MOVIES

The use of digital technologies has also had an impact on the movie industry, which has adopted digital tools for making and distributing movies. Since its beginnings, the movie industry has used film as the primary medium to record images. As discussed earlier, film cameras use a special technique to capture 24 frames of still images every second, which are later projected to show a moving image on the screen.

The adoption of digital technologies has happened in two important ways. Some movies have made extensive use of digital technologies to create special effects: A movie will be shot on film, and later, digital tools are used to create images that are added to the film version to create imaginary environments or fantastic creatures. A good example of this can be seen in the *Jurassic Park* trilogy, which involved real human beings interacting with creatures that were generated with digital tools. The combination of film and digital tools offers the opportunity to create very realistic special effects. The digitally generated images blend in well with the film images, offering an entertainment package that is visually pleasing.

Digital tools have also been used in producing movies created entirely with computer code, without ever using any film medium. This is the second way digital tools have impacted the movie industry. The movies most commonly created completely with a computer are animated ones. Each frame of the moving image is generated using special computer programs that are designed to create images similar to the traditional hand-drawn cartoons popularized by Disney.

A good early example of such a movie is *Toy Story*, released in 1995 by Pixar Studios. This movie marked a turning point in digital animation, as pointed out in 2005 by Burr Snider, a writer for *Wired*

Pictured is a scene from *The Lost World*, the sequel to *Jurassic Park*. The *Jurassic Park* series used computers to create computer-generated T. rexes and other dinosaurs. When filmmakers saw the imagery in *Jurassic Park*, they realized that many of the visions they thought were once impossible were now in reach.

magazine. "Each one of the movie's 1,560 shots was created on Silicon Graphics and Sun workstations by artists working from some 400 computer-generated mathematical models and backgrounds," Snider wrote. In this situation it is incorrect to call the movie a "film" since that medium was never used to create the animation. Later Pixar movies have continued to use computer-generated animation.

A variation to computer-generated animation movies are those that also use computer codes to create moving images, but do not restrict the images to cartoon characters. In 2001, Japanese director and producer Hironobu Sakaguchi created a movie called *Final Fantasy: The Spirits Within*. This movie used computer codes to create lifelike images of the human characters in the movie. The digital actors and actresses did not really exist. All the images were created using computer programs that were run on numerous powerful computers.

The latest example of this is James Cameron's *Avatar*, released in December 2009. Cameron, the writer and director of the film, created a whole world using computer technology. Cameron had announced in 1996 that he would be making the film, after he completed *Titanic* (which went on to become the highest-grossing film in the world). According to Cameron, digital technology was then not up to the task of being able to tell the story the way he wanted, so he waited until digital technology had advanced enough, in 2006. His partnership with visual effects house Weta Digital, owned by another master of the visual arts, Peter Jackson (writer, director, and producer of the Lord of the Rings movie series), used motion-capture technology to create a mythic, futuristic tale of blue people called Na'vi who are native to the planet Pandora. Cameron devised a new virtual camera that allowed him to observe on a video monitor how the actors' virtual counterparts interact with the film's digital world in real time and adjust as needed, like a director would do when shooting live action. "It's this form of pure creation where if you want to move a tree or a mountain or the sky or change the time of day, you have complete control over the elements," said Cameron, when talking about virtual filmmaking. He went on to describe the film as a hybrid of live-action combined with computer-generated characters and live environments. This type of filmmaking has not been done before, and audiences have gone out in droves to see the film. *Avatar* has topped *Titanic* to become the highest-grossing film of all time.

The development of realistic computer-generated stars is a phenomenon that could lead to a new form of movie making in which real actors and actresses could someday become obsolete. *New York Times* writer Ruth La Ferla pointed toward this trend in a 2001 article. "[T]hey have established personas of their own," she said of virtual movie characters, "and are able to migrate from one medium to another, building virtual careers much like flesh-and-blood beauties." The availability of powerful computers along with public acceptance of virtual characters could lead to increased use of these tools in future movie making.

DIGITAL DISTRIBUTION OF MOVIES

The process of making digital movies has been complemented by the development of tools that make it possible to distribute movies as digital files to both theaters and individual consumers. The traditional way of distributing movies has been through theaters outfitted with a film projector that required the movie to be sent on multiple reels of film. The film would then be fed into the projector, which would pass the film in front of a very bright lamp to project the image on the large screen. This method depended on the physical film as the primary mode of showing the movie. The image would look bad if the film was bad, and since most movies required multiple reels of films, it became important to have multiple projectors in each theater. That way, there could be a seamless transition from one reel to another. Some theaters would use a large platter to hold all the multiple reels so that one projector could be used to show the entire movie. In such cases the theater owner had to ensure that the different reels were correctly connected for projection and then cut up for return to the film distributor. This method also required multiple copies of the movie to be printed on many film rolls, which all had to be physically sent to the different movie theaters across the country and the world.

Many of the steps required for film distribution can be eliminated by sending the entire movie out as a digital file. The file can be placed on portable computer memory such as a DVD or computer hard drive. Then movie theaters would not need to handle reels of film but would instead use a computer and a powerful LCD projection system to display the image just as it would be displayed on a personal computer monitor. Movie theaters have to invest in the new form of projectors for this, but after the initial investment all movies can be shown using easily managed digital files. In addition, HD digital files have an extremely high number of pixels, which creates very sharp images on the large screen of a movie theater.

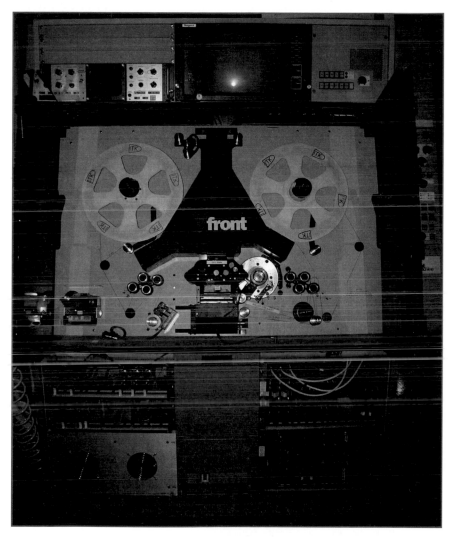

It takes a large amount of film to make a movie, about 2.13 miles (3.42 kilometers) for a typical two-hour movie. This equals five or six reels. It is also critical to have quality equipment, like this projector, in order to show it. In the past, theaters used the two-reel system, in which someone operated two projectors at the same time. The advent of the platter system in the 1960s, a device composed of two to four discs stacked vertically, brought about the supersize theater, or multiplex.

Although movies are usually distributed first in theaters, most movies also earn a significant amount of revenue through the sale and rental of DVDs. Many people prefer to wait a few months for a movie to be released on DVD and watch it in a home theater rather than going to a commercial movie theater. The volume of DVDs sold in 2008 amounted to a total of $14.5 billion. (This is actually a 19 percent drop, although DVD rentals remained steady at $7.5 billion and Blu-ray discs continued to gain in market share.) Moviemakers receive a portion of the rental or purchase cost of DVDs, adding to the overall profit of a movie. Some movies make more money from DVD sales and rentals than they do in the theater, as reported in *USA Today*.

Movie distribution with DVDs is a somewhat slow process and requires some effort on the part of the viewer. Someone who wants to watch a movie on DVD must either purchase the DVD or rent it. Some companies have made the process easier by renting out DVDs from their Web sites. One of the most popular of these companies is Netflix, which launched in 1999. Today it is the world's largest online movie rental service. For as little as $8.99 per month, depending on the price plan that is chosen, members have the privilege of browsing a large library of DVDs of television shows and movies and ordering whatever they want. They can even watch movies and television episodes on their home computers or TVs. Then they use a prepaid envelope to return the discs when finished. When Netflix was launched, film studios and distributors were concerned about the online movie rental company eating into the studios' profits. Now, with the weakened economy causing a reluctance among consumers to make DVD purchases, as well as the fast-growing rental service Redbox (15,000 kiosks are located at grocery stores and other locations around the country), which offers DVD rentals for $1, new concerns have arisen. On January 6, 2010, Netflix and Warner Bros. Home Entertainment announced a deal to make newly released Warner Bros. films available to Netflix subscribers for rental 28 days after release. Although Redbox kiosks have begun to cut into Netflix's profits, Netflix is actually better positioned to adapt to a delayed-rental strategy than companies like Redbox because most of Netflix's shipments to customers are catalog, or previously released, titles.

In addition, Warner Bros. titles will be available for streaming to Netflix customers. Streaming has become an increasingly important part of the company's strategy, with the number of subscribers streaming a film or TV episode from Netflix jumping 20 percent over the third quarter in 2009. Streaming is a method of distribution in which movies are stored as digital files on large, central computers that are connected to the Internet using very fast connections. People can purchase a membership with companies like Netflix that maintain these large databases of movies, and they can download a specific movie to the hard drives of their computers. Viewers can either watch the movies on the computer screen, or connect the computer to a large display device that produces a large picture. Downloading from the Internet offers a significant advantage over DVD rentals since the user can enjoy the movie instantly and can even watch it in parts because the digital file remains on the hard drive of the computer.

On January 7, 2010, Netflix announced at the annual Consumer Electronics Show in Las Vegas, Nevada, that it had made a deal to partner with five global consumer electronics companies to introduce Netflix-ready devices later in the year. These companies are Funai (which distributes Phillips, Magnavox, Sylvania, and Emerson in the United States), Panasonic, Sanyo, Sharp, and Toshiba. Each company will provide devices that will instantly stream thousands of movies and TV shows from Netflix to customers in the comfort of their homes. This deal is in addition to the Netflix-ready Blu-ray disc players available from Best Buy's Insignia brand, LG Electronics, Sony, and Samsung, as well as Microsoft's Xbox 360 and Sony's PlayStation 3, which instantly stream movies and TV episodes from Netflix.

Besides Redbox, rivals of Netflix include the Blockbuster store and the town library. As mentioned, Redbox is cheap and convenient—with more kiosks than traditional brick-and-

HD-DVD AND BLU-RAY

Movies were first released on DVD in 1997. The digital format used to store the image on a DVD provided image quality that was far superior to the popular videotape format that stored the image information on magnetic tapes. A limited amount of information could be stored on tape and the quality of the image decreased if the tape was damaged. The problem of image quality and longevity were both addressed with the development of the DVD. Still, the quality of the image stored on a DVD is not as good as the image that can be produced by HDTV technology. This drawback has led to research in developing a format and storage system that allows images to be stored at a level of detail matching the 1080p HD standard.

Two methods were developed simultaneously. One is called HD-DVD and was developed by Toshiba Corporation of Japan. The other is called Blu-ray DVD, developed by Sony Corporation of Japan. The two companies competed with each other, trying to ensure that its format would become more popular among viewers. One way this battle was fought was to produce computer games that used 1080p

mortar video stores in the country. Unlike Netflix, though, Redbox is unable to offer the selection and customer service that Netflix is known and admired for, so it has remained a far distant competitor. Blockbuster is a combination brick-and-mortar and mail service. While Blockbuster offers the most options—members can rent and return movies to the video store or have movies sent in the mail, with a guarantee that new movies will be in stock—it does not offer streaming options, which is where Netflix really excels. Online movie rental services combine the advantages of digital commerce with the ease of distribution offered by digital movies. Anyone can now rent a DVD as long graphics to enhance the games with dazzling images. Sony built the Blu-ray system into its PlayStation 3 game system and began to promote 1080p games, as well as market Sony movies on Blu-ray discs. The HD-DVD format was built into the Xbox 360 game system developed by Microsoft Corporation, and games were developed for the Xbox system using 1080p graphics.

By 2008, it was clear that the Blu-ray system was ahead in the competition, as more movie studios such as Warner Bros. announced that they would release their movies on the Blu-ray format as opposed to the HD-DVD format. Even though the Xbox game system is more popular than PlayStation 3, the endorsement from the movie industry helped to elevate the popularity of the Blu-ray system.

One important point to note about either one of the HD systems is that appropriate tools are needed to take full advantage of the quality of the picture. It is impossible to enjoy the full 1080p picture unless the display device is capable of handling that many pixels. An inferior display device will continue to produce a picture at the highest level of detail possible for it, which might not be the highest detail possible for the DVD format or the instrument used to play the DVD.

as he or she has Internet access and is willing to pay the membership and rental fee.

Lastly, one of the best deals for DVD distribution is the local library. Just about every town has a library and just about every library has DVD or VHS films for rent for a low cost or even for free. The selection may not be as up to date as the online movie rental services, but you cannot beat the price. Library movie rentals are particularly great for children's movies.

There is another method of DVD distribution that is gaining popularity. A digital movie file can be sent out using the same cables that bring digital HDTV to a home. These cables carry a digital signal from the cable company to the home, and the same cable can be used to send out other digital files. This process is used to provide specific television programming that the viewer has to pay for, often called pay-per-view programming. Since the program material exists in a digital format, it is possible for the user to purchase a single digital file for viewing without having to subscribe to an additional television channel. The user can scan through a series of movie titles, choose one, and begin watching it immediately. Since the movie arrives as a digital file, the user can manipulate the viewing experience by pausing the movie for a short time, fast-forwarding, or rewinding. This form of distribution is dependent on the availability of a cable connection. Consumers who don't subscribe to cable would not be able to take advantage of this method of distributing movies.

The digitization of moving images has offered some unique opportunities to the media industry. There are different ways of creating moving images, just as there are creative ways of distributing the digital file. The process of digitization also offers opportunities to individuals, who can now use the digital file to create personalized moving images.

Personal
Digital Video

The popularity of the digital video camera along with the availability of simple computer programs to manipulate digital video files has made it simple for ordinary people to create digital video. There are several different applications through which digital video enters a person's life.

Digital video cameras are now on sale at discount department stores such as Wal-Mart, and more people purchase these gadgets every day. Most personal computers are sold with computer programs that can be used to work with the digital video shot on these cameras. For example, every computer with the Windows operating system has a program called Windows Movie Maker. A user with a digital video camera can simply connect the camera to the computer and copy the digital video file to it. Then the user can make changes to the file, add special effects, overlay text onto the image, or combine it with sound effects to produce a final digital video file that could look quite professional. Most computers also have DVD

Originally used for television broadcasts, video cameras were large and heavy, mounted on special pedestals, and needed to be wired to remote recorders located in another room. Modern camcorders (video **cam**era re**corders**) can be used by anyone, are various sizes (some can even fit in the palm of your hand), are easy to use, and are inexpensive. Despite these advantages, camcorders now face competition due to the rising popularity of devices with basic video recording capability, like camera phones.

recorders that can be used to produce a DVD of this video file that can be viewed on a traditional video player. Many computers that are specially designed to be used as media processing tools also allow the user to add labels to DVDs that appear very professional. The combination of the digital video camera and the computer puts the power of producing effective digital video in the hands of any consumer who takes the trouble to learn some of the basic aspects of the technology.

The popularity of digital video is also seen in the fact that many cell phones can capture digital video. Although the quality of the moving images is not as good as what can be shot with a video camera, the video captured by a cell phone is quite adequate to keep a quick record of an important event. Sometimes a person might not have a video camera available, but since most people carry a cell phone, that tool can serve as a digital video recorder. In some cases, recordings done with a cell phone video camera become very important. There have been instances when mistreatment by police has been captured on cell phone digital video cameras and circulated globally to raise awareness about police brutality. For example, on June 11, 2009, Chicago police officer William Cozzi was sentenced to 40 months in prison for the 2005 beating of a man he had shackled to a wheelchair. Cozzi struck Randy Miles in front of others and the beating was caught on videotape.

There are also numerous ways that personal digital video can be distributed. Prior to the advent of digital video, personal memories were either recorded on film with 16 mm movie cameras, as discussed earlier, or on video cameras that stored the images on magnetic tape. Neither of these methods was convenient if the user wanted to make multiple copies of the files. It was too expensive to produce multiple film reels, and the process of video duplication degraded the quality of the image.

Digital video is far easier to copy since the process is no different from making multiple copies of a digital file. A digital video file can be copied an infinite number of times just as a digital text document can be copied over and over. There is no loss of quality in the video image as long as the copying process goes well. Computer programs can also be used to store the digital information in many formats for different kinds of use. Computer programs such as Windows Movie Maker offer the user more than a dozen ways to store the information: The user can choose to create a format that is suitable for transmission over the Internet, or the user can retain the best quality for copying the file onto DVDs.

The ability to create different formats allows the individual user to distribute the digital video in several ways. Family vacation

(continues on page 76)

YOUTUBE

The YouTube phenomenon was started in 2005 by Steve Chen, Chad Hurley, and Jawed Karim, former employees of a company called PayPal. YouTube offers its users an opportunity to share digital video through the YouTube Web site. People who have a registered account with YouTube can upload permitted video content that can be viewed worldwide. Only those who want to add video to the site need to register with it, and anyone can view the videos. The key to this technology is the use of Flash Video, which converts different kinds of video formats into a universal and standardized format that can be interpreted by any computer.

The process of video sharing offers people an opportunity to show their favorite images to people around the world. This process proved to be so attractive that, according to Quantcast, more than 91 million Americans visited the YouTube Web site in a single month in 2009. Many more visitors came from other parts of the world. People are watching hundreds of millions of video files a day, with hundreds of thousands being uploaded daily. In fact, according to YouTube, every minute 20 hours of video is uploaded to its Web site.

The kind of file added to YouTube and other video-sharing Web sites such as Google Video are usually not very long. Longer content is broken down into multiple smaller files. The smaller file size permits many users to watch the videos since no single file takes up too much of the available data channel used to transmit the digital files. When a viewer watches a YouTube video on a personal computer, the file is temporarily stored on the computer, and the user can choose to download specific files for future use.

YouTube has also been used by institutions for promoting specific ideas and agendas to a global audience. YouTube has often been used in political campaigning, with the promoters of certain politicians using the site to broadcast videos about their candidates. The 2008 U.S. presidential campaign witnessed numerous instances in which aides to the candidates, their supporters, and their opponents put videos on YouTube to either support their candidate or smear the opponent.

President Barack Obama's weekly radio address is viewed on a computer screen via YouTube.

The power of video sharing becomes clear when a nation feels compelled to stop its citizens from accessing YouTube, as reported in a 2008 article in the *New York Times:* "Internet users in China were blocked from seeing YouTube on Sunday after dozens of videos about protests in Tibet appeared on the popular American video Web site." Similar blocking has been reported from other countries, including Singapore and Pakistan.

Very few restrictions are placed on what can be sent to the YouTube Web site. Unless there are clear protests from specific groups, most of what is placed on the site is kept there. Sometimes there are protests based on copyrighted material. In 2007 the Japanese television system NHK forced YouTube to remove nearly 30,000 videos because they had been added without proper permission. YouTube also does not

(continues)

(continued)

allow offensive sexual material to be placed on the site, although there are other kinds of material that could be offensive to some viewers. One example of this is the case of racist cartoons depicting the days of segregation in the United States, as reported by Daniel E. Slotnik in a 2008 *New York Times* article: "Among the millions of clips on the video-sharing Web site YouTube are 11 racially offensive Warner Brothers cartoons that have not been shown in an authorized release since 1968." Although the material was later removed, these videos can crop up elsewhere once a digital version has been made available over the Internet. Other than some issues of copyright and offensive material, most of the millions of YouTube videos represent a positive way of sharing digital images.

(continued from page 73)

videos can be placed on DVDs and sent to different members of the family. The same video file can be placed on public Web sites that allow users to store the video file for others to watch. The video file can also be e-mailed to others who would be able to store the file on a personal computer and look at it. The availability of affordable tools to create and distribute digital video allows everyone with the right equipment to gain a voice in the public sphere if he or she wants to do so. It is no longer the case that only institutions are able to create moving images that are seen by a large number of people. Now, it is possible to place a digital video file on a shared Web site so that it is available to viewers worldwide. This allows more people to express their creative talents and share their opinions with many people.

Digital cameras make it possible for many people to create digital video. This empowers individuals with the ability to express themselves. There are other ways digital video plays a role in people's lives. The ability to manipulate digital video files allows people to better manage how media is used.

MEDIA TIME SHIFTING

John Fiske, an Australian media scholar, suggested in his 1987 book *Television Culture* that the popularity of television had led to people scheduling their days around their favorite programs. The television industry is clearly aware of this, since programming is designed in such a way as to attract the greatest audience numbers. The programs that are considered to be the most popular, such as certain sitcoms and reality shows, are broadcast in the early evening to attract the most viewers. The number of viewers is especially important since the programs that attract the largest audiences can also charge advertisers a higher price for commercial placement. Traditional television broadcasters assumed that viewers would adjust their schedules to watch television programs, and the accompanying advertisements, because there would be only a single opportunity to watch them.

The introduction of the videocassette recorder (VCR), which became popular in the early 1980s, offered viewers the opportunity to adjust the time they chose to watch a television program. Many viewers used the VCR to record a favorite show by programming the device to turn on and record when it came on. The viewer could later watch the show by replaying the taped program. After watching the show, the tape could be reused to record another show. The quality of the recording was dependent on the number of times a tape was used to record a show, and after several recordings the tape had to be discarded. The use of the VCR to record television programs was the beginning of the process of shifting the time when a person would watch a program, from the original broadcasted time to a time that was convenient to the viewer.

The introduction of digital technologies led to the replacement of the VCR by a device that could store the program as a digital file on a system similar to the hard drive of a personal computer. Some computer manufacturers such as Sony also started to sell computers in the early 2000s that had a built-in television receiver. With this, the user could connect a television antenna or cable directly into the computer, which could then record specified television programs. The process of using a computer as a tool to watch and record television programs became so popular by 2005 that Microsoft introduced a special operating system called Windows Media Center. This system offered a simple interface that people could use with a remote control to watch television and DVDs and listen to music

TIVO

The TiVo system was the brainchild of Jim Baron and Mike Ramsay and was introduced in 1997. The digital gadget was a superior replacement of the VCR that many people had been using as a time-shifting tool to record television programs and watch them at a later time. The same principle is repeated in the TiVo system, but at a digital level. Instead of using magnetic tapes to do the recordings, the TiVo system converts the video signal into a digital file and stores it on a magnetic hard drive similar to the hard drives used in computers. The TiVo unit is connected between the antenna or cable and the television set. The signal arriving through the cable is first interpreted by the TiVo unit and then sent on to the television. Based on instructions from the user, the TiVo unit is able to record specific shows and allows the user to watch them later.

The adoption of digital broadcasts over cable also allows television stations to send information about each show, just as the entire listing of programs is sent out by television broadcasters as digital data. The TiVo unit is able to interpret this data and offers the user the opportunity to schedule recordings of future shows. For example, a user can instruct the TiVo unit to record every program of a particular series for a certain length of time. Later, the viewer can watch the videos at leisure and can skip over the advertisements that accompany the programming.

The TiVo and related time-shifting devices could have a widespread impact on the way television programs are produced and dison the computer. The development of HDTV makes it even easier to record television programs as digital files because the program material is transmitted as digital information and the recorder simply has to copy it. The recorders are also powerful enough to record numerous hours of television programming. Some units are able to record up to 20 hours of programs in the HD format.

A study by the Carmel Group predicts that digital video recorders will be in 46 percent of U.S. households with televisions in 2010, for a total of 52.5 million units. Cable operators will provide 61 percent, satellite will provide 32 percent, with 6 percent provided by telephone/video providers and 2 percent by TiVo and others.

tributed. The ability to avoid advertisements has had an influence on the way companies try to advertise products and services on television. In a report published in 2004 on *CNET.com,* Stefanie Olsen noted, "A majority of national advertisers plan to cut spending on TV commercials by 20 percent in the next five years, when they believe that ad-skipping devices like TiVo will take hold in households." Advertisers are considering other ways to promote their products in places where they are more likely to be seen by the audience, because advertisements remain the primary way of financing television programs. The decreasing effectiveness of television advertisement will require stations to find other ways of supporting free television.

The ability to record a television program and then watch it later changes the way television might operate in the future everyday life of the audience. It is no longer necessary to have a rhythm of life that is partly dependent on television programs. It is possible to decide what programs are most attractive and then watch them at a time that is convenient to the viewer. It is also no longer necessary to watch the advertisements that accompany programs since it is easy enough to skip over the advertisements. When television programs are recorded on computer hard drives, it is also possible to transfer the programs to personal media players such as the iPod and watch them when commuting to work or waiting in a line. A television set is no longer required to watch programming because the digital content can be viewed on numerous other devices.

Television broadcasters have recognized all these changes in the television viewing habits of individuals. Many major television studios offer their popular programs as digital files that can be purchased from Web sites that sell media content. For example, Apple's iTunes Store, which sells much of the content for the iPod and iPhone media players, also offers many television programs that can be downloaded for viewing on personal media players.

The digitization of media content has changed the way media is watched. Today's viewer has a great deal of control over what programs are watched and when. The viewer can also create a unique sequence of programs that is based entirely on personal preference, as compared to what television broadcasters feel is a good sequence of programs.

PERSONALIZED MEDIA

There has been a growth in personalizing the media viewing experience as digital video has become increasingly commonplace. Much commercial video is easily digitized in many formats suitable for a range of devices, from projectors that can display a large image to tiny personal media players that a user can carry around easily. There has also been the development of video playlists, similar to music playlists, that allow individuals to create a customized set of videos that only includes shows that interest the viewer. With the availability of different devices that can be used to watch video, there is no longer a need to watch shows in the order they appear on television.

The arrangement of shows on television follows a pattern that has existed since the popularity of television began in the 1950s. In the United States this flow of television programs is made up of morning talk shows, afternoon game shows and soap operas, early evening news programs, evening sitcoms, dramas, and reality shows, and finally late-night shows that are meant for an audience of people over 18 years of age. This programming format was quite effective before the development of TiVo technology and the availability of videos on the Internet.

Starting in the early 2000s people were no longer restricted to television as the primary source of videos. The adoption of digital video offered the viewer numerous ways of personalizing the content as well as a great deal of choice in terms of the different sources from which the content would be obtained. Digital video files are available for download from the Internet and for purchase or rental in DVD format. All of this provides easy ways of watching digital video. The viewer also has many devices on which a combination of video files can be placed to be watched in a particular sequence. Digital video can be stored on tiny devices such as the iPod or can be obtained as a streaming file on a networked cell phone. Commercial video is available through Web sites that sell such content, but it is also possible to obtain digital files from amateur video producers who might have created an interesting video and placed it for public viewing on a video-sharing Web site.

The process of personalization leads to a significant change in the way video operates in culture. It is no longer the case that everyone has to watch the same set of television programs at the exact time the show is broadcast. With digital video, every person could potentially produce a unique combination of shows that only he or she likes. Digital video makes it possible for the viewer to watch these videos numerous times whenever and wherever. The basic foundation of mass communications, which is built on the fact that the same message can reach a large number of people, is questioned when every person can potentially create a unique program lineup. This move toward personalization also makes it difficult to ensure that all video files are appropriately protected from copyright infringement, leading to a significant loss of income for those who spend money to produce the videos. This issue will be discussed in the following chapter.

Working with Digital Video

A digital video file is no different from a digital text file. Both kinds of files exist as binary data that is stored on computer hard drives, and it is possible to make multiple copies of them. The digital video file can also be shared with others using a network connection because it can be sent from one computer to another just as easily as any other digital file can be shared.

When a digital file is created, the file itself always remains as digital data. It is possible to create copies of this digital data so all its binary number information is transferred to a new file that can be viewed with a different computer. The process is very different from the way video was copied with VCRs. In that case, the entire magnetic information stored on the cassette tape had to be transferred to a new tape. The transfer was done by first converting the magnetic information from the tape into electrical signals that were used to create a new set of magnetic information on another tape. The conversion to electrical signals and the reconversion to magnetic information always led to a lowering of the quality of the copy. If more copies were made from the first copy, they would be of even worse quality.

This problem does not exist in the case of the digital file, which can be copied digit by digit into a new file. As long as all the original digits are retained, it is possible to create an image that is identical to the original. A viewer is unable to recognize a copy from an original because each comes from the same set of digital information.

The conversion/reconversion process required with tape also needed to happen in real time. For example, if the original material had 20 minutes of video, then it would take 20 minutes to make a copy on tape. This made copying a time-consuming process. The digital copying process, however, is dependent on how rapidly the computer can do computations, since information about the image rather than the actual image is being copied. A fast computer can quickly do the necessary computations and copy the digital information from one hard drive to another. For example, a file containing 20 minutes worth of video can be copied in less than 5 minutes. The speed of copying makes the process much more efficient than former methods of duplicating moving images.

Digital video can also be copied on many kinds of media. In the era of VCRs, video could only be copied on different kinds of magnetic tape. Most tapes were large in size and were cumbersome to carry around. The most amount of video that could be copied on a tape is also restricted to about six hours of medium-quality video images. A digital file containing video information can be copied on any storage device that can hold binary data. The hard drive of a computer is the best example of such a storage system. Computers now could hold hundreds of hours worth of video when compressed and copied with medium levels of detail. A single DVD, which is much more portable than videocassettes, can easily hold a full-length feature film at very high levels of detail, or up to six feature films when copied at lower levels of quality. A digital video file can also be copied onto personal media players. The iPod can hold about 75 hours worth of video files.

These memory devices can be reused many times without any loss in the quality of the storage device. It is also possible to constantly update the videos on a personal media player by deleting older video files and replacing the deleted files with recent files. The ability to store digital video files in many formats and on different devices makes it especially easy to produce many immaculate duplicates and then distribute them widely. This capability has also made it easy for the illegal reproduction of digital video. The unscrupulous merchants who engage in this practice are often called pirates because they steal the video for personal profit.

PIRACY OF DIGITAL VIDEO

There are two primary ways in which video piracy works. Once a video has been converted to a digital file, it is possible to make numerous copies of it on DVD and sell those copies. It is also

Not only does piracy affect those employed in Hollywood, there are "invisible" victims as well. In July 2009, an organized crime group was found guilty of keeping hundreds of Chinese workers in virtual slavery for years as part of a multi-million-dollar pirate DVD industry in the United Kingdom. Above, a customer looks through DVDs at a street stall selling pirated video games and DVDs in India.

possible to place a digital video file on a Web site so that visitors to the site can download the entire file to a personal computer. Both methods are used by video pirates, resulting in huge losses to the movie industry worldwide. An analysis by the Motion Pictures Association of America (MPAA) showed that nearly $6 billion was

HOW THE PIRATE WORKS

The success of a digital video pirate depends on how quickly a digital product is made available in the marketplace and the quality of the digital video. If a high-quality digital video file is released as soon as, or before, a movie is released in the theater, then it is quite likely that a large number of people will purchase the pirated product. New digital technologies make it easy for pirates to release high-quality videos very quickly.

The process begins with converting a moving image into a digital file. Most movies shown in theaters worldwide are still delivered on film. Large reels of film are sent to many movie theaters and these film reels are loaded up for projection on the screen. A pirate often works with unscrupulous theater operators who allow the pirates to have access to the film in order to create a digital copy of the movie. This is often done with a tool called the Telecine, which could vary in price from several hundred dollars to about $10,000. The Telecine machine allows the pirate to run the film reel through the machine and create a digital file of the movie. Digital video of very high quality can be produced with a good Telecine machine, providing the pirate a perfect digital copy of the movie. This can later be copied onto DVDs for sale or placed on a Web site for downloads. Since the Telecine is an expensive investment, most pirates use a different method for creating digital copies.

The most common form of piracy is done with the help of a digital video camera that is taken inside a movie theater. The entire movie is recorded by the digital camera. This copy of the movie is then distributed. This method does not produce a very good copy of the image and the pirated video is lost to video pirates in 2005, and 90 percent of all the videos sold in China were illegal versions.

The legality of a video is related to who produces the digital file. When a movie is legally released on DVD after the movie has played in theaters, the DVD is sold in legitimate stores for a price

only available after the movie has been released in theaters. Once the digital copy is produced, it can be easily distributed globally, even to places where the movie might not yet have been released in theaters.

Pirates take advantage of the fact that movies are released in a staggered way across the globe. For example, a movie might be released in the United States at the end of May, but the same movie might not be available in India until the end of June. Pirates use that month to rapidly sell illegal copies to the huge Indian population, which would already have heard about the movie through Web sites and other Internet resources. By the time the movie is legally released in India, a large part of the population might have seen the pirated version of the movie in their homes. This is why the Motion Picture Association of America and other similar organizations are trying to coordinate the release of movies in such a way that the pirates do not have sufficient time to make a profit.

Sellers of pirated DVDs do not operate in regular stores. Instead, they often sell their wares in large cities through temporary kiosks or even just on blankets laid on the ground. The sellers of the pirated products are very skilled at quickly hiding their products if there is a threat from the police. For example, a BBC report in 2004 described how pirated DVDs are sold in shopping malls in Britain: "Men appeared with a blanket and began laying out a range of DVDs—including two copies of *Spider-Man 2* on display." These sellers do not need an elaborate shop or advertising to sell their products, allowing them to sell the DVDs for a cheap price while still making a hefty profit. The consumer can buy a product of reasonable quality for a fraction of the price in a store. This makes it especially difficult to curb the growth of piracy.

determined by the studio. A movie on DVD could cost up to $40 in a store. The proceeds from the movie bring in profits to all the different players involved in making it, from the studio executives to the writers of the screenplay. Releasing the movie on DVD after its theatrical run also ensures that more people will go to a movie theater to watch the movie instead of watching it in a home theater.

The video pirate often makes a movie available as a digital file before the movie has had its theatrical run. Unscrupulous movie industry workers make early copies of the video available to pirates, who create the digital version of the video and then release copies of it. For example, in a 2008 *Financial Express* report from India, which produces more films than any other country in the world, journalist Soma Das wrote, "Most Hindi and regional films succumb to piracy before release, while foreign films are largely pirated in a movie theatre."

One of the biggest threats to the movie industry is the availability of pirated movies before their theatrical release dates, since a large portion of the audience would be lost if digital video of good quality is available before the movie appears in theaters. In an interview with *USA Today* in 2003, John Fithian, president of the National Association of Theatre Owners, was concerned by the way the work of pirates could impact the profitability of movie theaters.

The most curious part of the pirating phenomenon is that it exists because there is a large group of consumers who are willing to buy the illegal product. Although there is a lack of systematic studies that explore the primary reasons for this, there is some evidence to suggest that the most important factor supporting piracy is the price of the digital video. The pirated product is far less expensive than the legitimate product. The price advantage makes the pirated product more attractive to consumers who are unwilling or unable to pay the normal price for a DVD or a ticket at a movie theater.

The price motivation has been true from the early days of piracy, when digital tools made it possible to quickly make copies of different kinds of digital files. In a 1995 article in the *New York Times,* journalist Michael Specter describes the piracy industry in Russia. In Moscow, "[n]early every kiosk, stall, store, or market in the city sells videocassettes, compact discs, and computer software at prices that would make any American customer reach for his or her wallet," he writes.

The price advantage comes from the fact that pirates steal the original digital file and then rapidly make DVD copies of it or release it on the Internet. The pirates do not have to bear the huge costs of making the movie, but still reap the benefits of the product. Uncontrolled piracy could eventually cripple the legitimate movie industry because theoretically the industry would not make enough profit to sustain itself and thus wither away. In a strange twist of fate, the pirates would have nothing to sell if that were to happen.

Digital tools have made the work of pirates simpler. It is up to the consumer to decide if he or she will support the stolen product or the legitimate product. This decision would be simpler if the legitimate media industry provided the goods at a price comparable to what is offered by the pirates. The industry's profits might seemingly be lowered by doing this, but the pirates would be put out of business. Piracy continues to grow because of the price advantage and also because digital video tools are becoming easily available to large numbers of people.

DIGITAL VIDEO FOR PERSONAL USE

As discussed earlier, the easy availability of digital video cameras has made it possible for individuals to produce and distribute digital files through YouTube and other video-sharing Web sites. These tools allow individuals to gain a voice and say what they want, giving them a role in mass communications.

Digital video is also playing a role in how two people interact with each other over long distances. The telephone is one tool for long-distance interpersonal communication, but the disadvantage is that the people talking are unable to see each other. There has been a long-standing interest in developing interpersonal communication tools that allow people to see each other as well. Starting in the late 1950s, research teams at Bell Laboratories were interested in developing a system that would allow callers to see each other on a small video screen. The product was called the PicturePhone and was briefly sold to some customers in Chicago, but it soon disappeared because of the cumbersome and expensive tools required to operate the system.

The idea of transmitting pictures reappeared when video signals could be easily converted into digital files able to be sent over the Internet. Since data can travel very rapidly over the Internet, it is possible to instantly send a digital video file from one computer to another. Depending on the equipment used, the quality of the picture is sometimes not very good, but it is possible for the two people to see each other while talking. There is no need for a special device to show the picture, since a computer screen could be used. The miniaturization of video cameras also means that a small camera is all that is needed to capture a video.

These different technological developments have led to the popularity of using video on a computer as the primary tool of communication. One example of such a system is Voice over Internet Protocol (VoIP), which turns a computer into a phone. The VoIP system allows people to make calls from one computer to another over the Internet. The sound is sent as digital files from one computer to the other. Since most digital files are similar in nature, the system that supports the VoIP process can also transmit digital video files over the same connection, making it possible to use the system for digital video transmission as well.

One of the most popular providers of global VoIP is a company called Skype, which allows users to speak for free over great distances. In 2005 the company started to offer Skype Video, a program that allows any of the millions of Skype users to see each other when making a call. The ability to see the other person could change the nature of conversations and make it possible for people

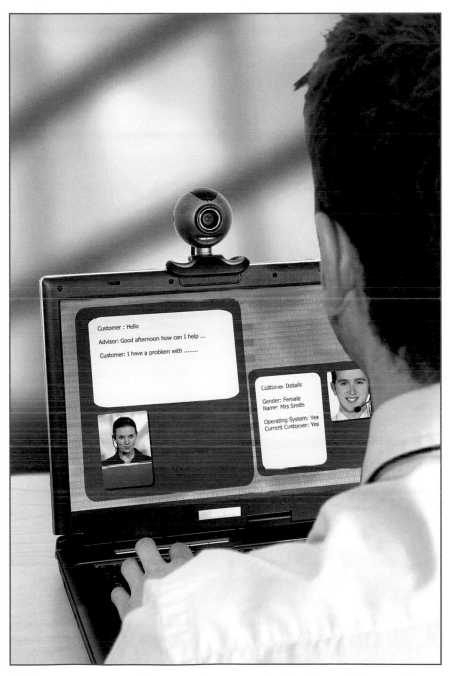

Webcams are a popular way of communicating long distance. These devices are used for entertainment purposes, for law enforcement, and for business. Above, this customer service representative has an online chat with a customer via webcam and headsets.

to remain better connected using communication tools that make the best use of digital video.

Personal digital video also shows up in the use of personal Web-based cameras that constantly send a picture from a camera to a Web site so that people can easily monitor what might be going on at a remote location. This is a form of surveillance camera that is used by an individual as opposed to a government or the police. Tiny digital video cameras can be placed at different locations throughout a home so that they all connect with a computer over a local network. The user can see the picture from each camera on the computer screen. One industry that has taken advantage of this technology offers digital video monitors to parents who want to keep an eye on a child sleeping in a different room. Baby monitors have been popular in developed countries since the availability of the miniature radio in the 1950s, but the development of digital technologies allows for the addition of video to the traditional audio monitor.

The key to the use of personalized digital cameras is in the fact that they can connect directly with other computers on a network and offer a constant stream of digital video data. This information can be placed on the Internet, allowing anyone to watch the video from a distance. At the personal level, this offers the opportunity to monitor specific locations from a distance. It also means that people can choose to set up a constant stream of digital video data that anyone can watch as long as they have access to the appropriate Web site.

Such cameras are called webcams. The first such camera was used in 1991 by students of computer science at Cambridge University in Britain. The digital camera was set up to constantly send out pictures of a coffee pot in a kitchen, showing the amount of coffee in the pot. Anyone wanting coffee would be able to see on a computer screen how much coffee was available before deciding to walk over to get some.

This concept of a constant stream of digital video available on the Internet was especially popularized by Jennifer Kaye Ringley of Harrisburg, Pennsylvania. Ringley set up several cameras in her home between 1996 and 2003, allowing anyone to watch what was happening in her personal life. This experiment, named JenniCam,

In the past, baby monitors consisted of two walkie-talkie-like devices that often experienced interference from other wireless devices or had low auditory capabilities due to static. Modern baby monitors have come a long way. Today, digital baby monitors are resistant to interference, have long-range capability, and have an LCD screen so that parents can view their baby when they are not in the same room.

gained widespread popularity. Several other people started to display their own lives on the Internet. A 1999 *New York Times* article reported on numerous other cameras such as PuppyCam to show dogs, CatCam to show cats, and KremlinCam to show what was happening at the Kremlin in Moscow, Russia. The emergence of digital video has allowed individuals to find a way to have their personal stories seen by a large global audience.

The Future of Digital Video

This book has examined some of the key components of digital video, which has become the principal way that people produce moving images in the twenty-first century. Most of the moving images produced in popular culture, both by professionals and amateurs, have some amount of digital video in them. For example, the 2008 movie *Indiana Jones and the Kingdom of the Crystal Skull* was mostly based on digital video, while the earlier movies of the same series used no digital effects at all. The movie retained the look of the earlier films but created that look using digital effects. Such trends point toward a sophistication of digital video technology that can produce images that might not look digital at all but are used for "creating realistic-yet-fantastic environments and creatures," as described in a 2008 CNN news report about the Indiana Jones movie.

The adoption of digital video in everyday life has been facilitated by the availability of numerous digital video tools. There are many gadgets that can be used to capture digital video images, just as there are numerous ways of displaying the images. At the same time, there is an increasing presence of digital video on the Internet that has become globally accessible. Connections to the Internet have become faster, allowing people to easily transfer digital video files using the Internet. Web sites such as YouTube have made it easy for people to instantly send video images from a personal camera to a global audience. The combination of the ease of producing and broadcasting video images poses a series of challenges for the future, particularly with respect to the way digital video images could be used (or abused) both by institutions and individuals.

Digital video taken on small cameras is being used in many ways. For example, in 2007 a set of trial lawyers won its case using video footage of hate images produced by a church in Kansas. A 2008 news report in the *Law Technology News* described how videos were used in the trial: "Plaintiffs used the footage to show the outrageous nature of the church's message." Such use of digital video could become more common as video capturing devices are installed in many locations and it becomes easier to capture digital images for future use—or even instant use. In 2008 a company called Pure Digital actively marketed a product called the Flip, a pocket-sized digital video camera that could be connected directly to a computer to send the captured video immediately to Web sites such as YouTube.

It is also now possible to store large volumes of digital information that could be used to track specific habits of people. In addition to that, it is possible to match digital images of people with other databases that might include old digital images. For example, some airline companies such as Southwest Airlines have installed digital cameras on their aircrafts to monitor the activity of the passengers to detect any suspicious activity suggesting terrorist action. When the information is captured as digital video, the images can be used for comparison with databases of existing video of known terrorists to ensure that a criminal is not on the plane. Although the tool can

In order to increase security and deter crime, London, England, has installed surveillance cameras throughout the city. The CCTV User Group estimates that there are about 1.5 million closed-circuit television cameras in city centers, stations, airports, retail stores, and other public places, reportedly more cameras per person than in any other country. The number of cameras has triggered concerns about privacy. Above, a police officer watches a television monitor in the Metropolitan Police's Special Operations Room in London.

prevent a disaster, it also could lead to compromising the privacy of all the other passengers on a plane. With the increasing use of digital surveillance cameras, such issues of privacy are likely to become more critical.

The ease with which digital video can be copied and distributed also gives rise to issues related to its misuse. The primary concern is with piracy of digital entertainment material. That problem will only become worse as personal computers become more powerful and anyone with the right tools is able to make perfect copies of digital video from DVDs and distribute them quickly over the

Internet. The way to reduce this behavior would be to change the way video is distributed by corporations that produce movies and television shows. To many consumers, the pirated version of the video offers a much cheaper way to watch the material, even if the video is of inferior quality.

It is possible that piracy would decline when the legitimate distributors of video are able to provide a high-quality video image at a reasonable price. Some companies are beginning to do this by offering videos through their Web sites. For example, NBC allows viewers to watch selected episodes of some television shows on its Web site. Companies such as Movielink are also offering registered users the opportunity to legally download movies for home viewing. Such developments could allow users to gain access to a large amount of digital video material without turning to pirates.

Opportunities like those offered by NBC and Movielink also point toward another important future trend in digital video: individuals being able to personalize the video content that they watch. The rapid adoption of HDTV and the availability of video from the Internet, along with the use of devices like TiVo, allow viewers to decide exactly what kind of content they want to watch and when they want to watch it. The popularity of gadgets such as the iPod poses a further challenge to the existing economic structure of television broadcasts that make money through advertising. The personalization of television-viewing habits would require stations to reconsider the way programs are funded and advertisers to reconsider how products could be marketed. This is a trend that will change as more people become accustomed to personalizing their viewing habits.

The general industrial trend and the popularity of digital video suggest that there will be growing use of this technology in the future. It would benefit the user to be knowledgeable about the technology and the appropriate use of the tools of digital video.

Chronology

3100 B.C.	Numbers with 10 base used in Egypt.
A.D. **628**	Indian mathematician Brahmagupta suggests that zero was a real number and offers rules for its use.
1040	Printing press developed in China by the Chinese inventor Bi Sheng, who carved Chinese characters with wood.
1200	The abacus is used to do mathematical calculations in China.
1439	Johannes Gutenberg develops the printing press in Europe.
1666	The idea of the binary number system using zero and one is introduced.
1822	Charles Babbage designs the first mechanical computer, using the idea of binary numbers.
1876	Alexander Graham Bell patents the first telephone.
1904	John Fleming makes the vacuum tube that can be used as an electronic switch.
1923	Interpol established as an international police force to fight international crime.
1927	*The Jazz Singer* is released as the first movie to use sound.
1947	John Bardeen builds the transistor that replaces the vacuum tube.

1948   Howard Aiken develops an electronic computer with 5,000 vacuum tubes.

Patent issued for Cathode Ray Tube Amusement Device, starting the era of digital games.

1953   IBM introduces the model 604 computer with transistors.

1956   IBM introduces the magnetic hard drive as a storage medium.

1957   IBM introduces the model 608 computer for the commercial market.

1964   John Kemeny and Thomas Kurtz develop the BASIC computer program language.

1967   The analog sound generator Moog synthesizer is adopted by rock band the Monkees.

1969   DARPA funds the development of an international network of computers.

The lunar module lands on the moon, using a computer smaller in capacity than a personal computer of 2009.

1970   Digital Electronics Corporation introduces the personal dot matrix printer.

1975   Industrial Lights & Magic established by George Lucas to use computer graphics in making movies.

Byte magazine is launched as the first magazine dealing with digital technology.

The PLATO networked education system serves 146 locations in Illinois.

1977   Apple Corporation introduces the Apple II computer.

1978   Roy Trubshaw, a student at Essex University in the United Kingdom, starts working on a multiuser adventure game called *MUD* (*Multiuser Dungeon*).

1980	Polydor Company of Hanover, Germany, produces the commercially available compact disc.
	Pac-Man game released in Japan.
1981	Microsoft develops the DOS computer program as the operating system for computers.
	IBM introduces the first personal computer using the MS-DOS operating system.
1982	The Groupe Spécial Mobile (GSM) cell phone technology is developed by the Conference of European Posts and Telecommunications (CEPT).
	The compact disc is introduced in the United States.
1985	Intel introduces the 80386 microprocessor, with 275,000 transistors built into the chip.
	The computer program WELL is set up to allow a community of people to exchange computer files with one another.
	The C++ computer language is released commercially.
1986	The Farooq Alvi brothers, operating out of Lahore, Pakistan, release the first computer virus called "The Brain."
1987	German scientist Dieter Seitzer develops the mp3 format for digitizing sound.
1989	The European Center for Particle Research (CERN) in Switzerland invents the World Wide Web.
	SimCity developed as an alternative to shoot-up digital games.
	Nintendo introduces the Game Boy in the United States.
1990	Commercially available digital still camera sold by Logitech.

Code Division Multiple Access (CDMA) cell phone technology is developed by Qualcomm.

1992   First Short Message Service (SMS) message sent from a cell phone.

1993   Intel introduces the Pentium microprocessor, with 3.1 million transistors built into the chip.

Researchers at the University of Illinois at Urbana-Champaign introduce Mosaic as a tool to browse data on the Web.

1995   *Toy Story* is produced by using only computer-generated images to create a complete movie.

Presidential Savings Bank is the first bank to provide the option of doing financial transactions on the computer.

Pierre Omidyar, a French-born Iranian computer scientist, establishes the prototype for the online auction Web site eBay.

1996   Health Insurance Portability and Accountability Act (HIPAA) is introduced, placing strict regulations about who may have access to the health information of Americans.

Palm introduces the personal digital assistant (PDA).

Travelocity.com launches an online system for selling airline tickets.

1997   The digital video disc (DVD) is introduced in the United States.

Movies begin to be released on DVDs.

TiVo is introduced to digitally capture television shows.

Instant Messaging (IM) technology is introduced by companies like America Online (AOL).

"Deep Blue" computer beats Garry Kasparov at chess.

1998   The United States adopts the Digital Millennium Copyright Act (DMCA), which offers extensive legal protection to the creators and distributors of digital products.

Printed version of *Byte* is discontinued after 23 years in publication, having been the first magazine to deal with digital technologies.

New Media & Society is launched by Sage Publications to examine the role of digital technologies in society.

The Motion Picture Experts Group standardizes the MP4 format for capturing and storing digital video.

Google begins with a $100,000 investment as a company operating from a garage.

2000   Nearly 5,000 satellites are in space.

Trek Technology and IBM introduce the flash memory as a storage medium.

Google becomes the most popular Internet search tool.

2001   Apple introduces the iPod.

Wikipedia is launched as a freely editable online encyclopedia.

2003   Linden Research Laboratories introduces Second Life as a multiuser social game.

United Nations Educational, Scientific and Cultural Organization (UNESCO) begins a special award on digital art through their "DigiArts" mission.

MySpace is introduced as a social networking Web site.

2004   Two-thirds of Americans claim to use instant messaging on a regular basis.

Liberated Syndication offers the first podcast hosting service for a $5 monthly fee.

Revenue from the sale of digital games doubles from the 1994 sales level.

The Food and Drug Administration (FDA) approves the use of an embedded microprocessor in the human body for medical purposes.

2005 Steve Chen, Chad Hurley, and Jawed Karim introduce YouTube.

In one of the largest breaches of the security of personal information, 40 million Visa and MasterCard credit card numbers become available to anyone on the Internet.

Ninety percent of all videos sold in China are illegally produced pirated copies of the original DVD.

Microsoft introduces the Xbox 360 game system.

In the United States, the number of identity thefts exceeds 250,000.

Google introduces Google Maps as a digital mapping tool.

2006 Eleven years after its launch, eBay has 200 million registered users worldwide.

Sony introduces the PlayStation3 game system.

Nintendo introduces the Wii game system.

Sun Microsystems releases Java as a computer program that anyone can freely use.

Facebook becomes available to anyone in the world.

In Britain, the number of surveillance cameras reaches 4.2 million, 1 for every 14 people.

On average, the number of spam e-mails sent per day reaches 12.4 billion.

2007 In a single month, more than 24 million users visit the YouTube Web site.

American consumers spend about $30 billion shopping on the Internet during the Christmas shopping season.

Sales of the LCD screen surpass sales of the CRT screen worldwide.

Apple introduces the iPhone.

James Cameron and Vince Pace develop the 3-D Fusion Camera System to shoot feature films in stereoscopic 3-D. It is used to shoot several films, including *Aliens of the Deep*, *The Adventures of Sharkboy and Lavagirl*, and *Ghosts of the Abyss*.

2008 The number of airline tickets sold on the Internet exceeds the number sold through travel agents and other offline systems.

2009 All television stations in the United States begin broadcasting digital signals.

2010 James Cameron's film *Avatar*, which is made almost entirely of computer-generated animation using the 3-D Fusion Camera System, breaks the record for highest-grossing film of all time. It is also the first movie ever to earn more than $2 billion worldwide.

Glossary

America Online (AOL) A private company providing Internet access for a fee.

analog A signal that delivers data continuously in time and amplitude; can be converted into a digital signal.

Apple Corporation A private company manufacturing digital goods.

archive A collection of historical records of information.

Atari A private company manufacturing digital game products.

binary system A system that represents numeric values using only two digits, usually zero and one.

Bose Corporation A private company manufacturing audio systems like speakers.

British Broadcasting Corporation (BBC) The state-owned radio and television broadcasting organization in Great Britain.

broadband A method of sending digital information that allows a large amount of information to be sent in a short time.

buffer A temporary space where digital information can be stored for a short period while the computer processes the information.

C++ language A widely used computer programming language used in a large range of applications.

Center for Disease Control (CDC) An American government agency that is concerned with the health and safety of people.

chat room A type of computer program available on the Internet that allows several people to communicate with one another in real time.

compact disc (CD) A storage medium for music or computer data.

computation A specific mathematical operation, such as an addition or subtraction, performed by a digital tool like a cell phone.

computer code A series of letters and numbers that makes up the instructions given to a computer.

computer monitor A device that acts as the interface between the user and the computer, showing the texts and images produced by the computer.

computer program A series of commands given to a computer, instructing the computer to perform a series of tasks.

data storage system A way to permanently save large amounts of digital information.

digital A quantity, measurement, or signal represented by a series of discrete numbers; an analog signal can be converted into a digital one by sampling its value at periodic intervals.

digitize The process of converting a continuous quantity, having a numerical value at each instant, to a quantity represented by discrete numbers.

download A process of moving digital information from a centralized repository of data to a personal digital device like a personal computer.

electron An atomic particle having a negative charge; currents flowing in many conductors, such as metals, consist primarily of electrons in motion.

electronic bulletin board A computer program that allows group members to send information to a centralized computer so that all group members can access the information.

Entertainment Software Rating Board (ESRB) A self-regulatory American organization that calibrates entertainment products like computer games and other digital entertainment products based on suitability for different age groups.

fiber-optic line A cable that uses pulsating light to transmit digital information.

forum   A computer program that allows a group of people to exchange digital information by placing the information on a centralized computer accessible to all group members.

Game Boy   The trademark of a handheld digital device used for playing digital games.

handheld controller   A portable device, like a small remote control, that is used to control the operations of a digital device.

handheld game machine   A portable digital device that is used to play digital games.

hard drive   A device that is used in digital machines to store information.

high-speed connection   Same as BROADBAND, a method of sending digital information that allows a large amount of information to be sent in a short time.

intellectual property   A legal right of ownership over the creations of the mind, such as music, art, literature, and scientific ideas.

interactive   Describing a process in which every step of the process is dependent on the previous step, as in the case of a conversation in which each message is based on what was just said.

International Business Machine (IBM)   A multinational company that pioneered the manufacture of a computer for personal use.

Internet   The connection of numerous computers where each computer can interact with any other computer on the network.

Java   A special type of computer program that has become very popular for use with Web sites, because the programs can be interpreted by any kind of computer.

keyboard   A device that has a button for every letter of an alphabet and is used by computer users to interact with computers.

local area network (LAN)   A connection between computers that are spatially close to each other, as in the case of a set of computers in a private home.

Magnavox An American company specializing in the manufacture of home electronic products like televisions, radios, and DVD players.

memory A component in a digital device that is used to store information, both for long periods of time and short periods of time while the device does computations.

microprocessor A component in a digital device that contains microscopic electronic switches that are etched onto a tiny piece of silicon, making up the most important part of all digital devices.

Microsoft An American company that produces the Windows operating systems used in computers worldwide.

mouse A device used with a computer to simulate the movement of a pointer on the computer screen by moving the physical point ing device on a flat surface.

nationality The identity of a person based on a person's citizenship documents, such as passports.

networked A process that connects different digital devices with each other.

networked environment A working condition where many different digital devices are connected to one another.

Nintendo A Japanese company that manufactures and sells hand-held computer games, devices, and digital game systems.

Nintendo DS A more advanced version of GAME BOY.

nodal computer A machine that makes up the center of a network of computers.

personal computer (PC) A machine that can be used by a single individual as a personal computer to perform many different digital tasks.

personal digital assistant (PDA)   A handheld digital device that keeps a record of contacts, appointments, tasks, and other personal information.

platform   The fundamental computer program, like WINDOWS, that provides the support for a large range of computer programs.

PlayStation   A personal digital gaming device created by Sony that has the characteristics of a personal computer and also contains a built-in high-definition DVD player.

process   A specific set of tasks that a digital device performs to provide a specific function like large statistical calculations.

refresh   The way in which the image on a COMPUTER MONITOR is periodically updated to reflect changes in information sent to the computer.

shooting games   A category of digital games that uses a replica of a gun or cannon to shoot at objects on the screen.

Sony   A Japanese company specializing in the manufacture of home electronic products such as computers, televisions, radios, and DVD players.

statistics   A special branch of mathematics focusing on creating estimates and trends by looking at a large amount of data about a specific phenomenon.

text-based message   A form of communication that uses only letters of the alphabet.

virtual   Any system or phenomenon that only exists as a digital file without any tangible component.

web-based magazine   A category of publications that does not have a paper version but exists only on the Internet.

Web   The short and colloquial term for the World Wide Web computer program that uses a universal computer language to exchange different kinds of digital information among computers connected to the Internet.

Wii   A personal digital gaming created by Nintendo that uses wireless, motion-controlled remotes.

Xbox   A personal digital gaming device created by Microsoft that has the characteristics of a personal computer and also contains a built-in high-definition DVD player.

Bibliography

Bell, Donald. "Apple iPod Classic (80GB, silver)." *Cnet.reviews*, September 7, 2007. Available online. URL: http://reviews.cnet.com/mp3-players/apple-ipod-classic-80gb/4505-6490_7-32595955.html.

Bowman, D. A. and R. P. McMahan. "Virtual Reality: How Much Immersion Is Enough?" *Computer* vol. 40, no. 7 (July 2007) 36–43.

Cripps, Dale. "President Bush Signs Historic DTV Bill, CEA Says HDTV Is on a Roll." *HDTV Magazine*, February 8, 2006. Available online. URL: http://www.hdtvmagazine.com/articles/2006/02/president_bush_signs_historic_dtv_bill_cea_says_hdtv_is_on_a_roll.php.

Das, Soma. "Hindi Movie Pirates Steal Show before Launch." *The Financial Express*, April 2, 2008. Available online URL: http://www.financialexpress.com/news/hindi-movie-pirates-steal-show-before-launch/291263.

Hafner, Katie. "Drawn to the Hearth's Electronic Glow." *New York Times*, January 24, 2002. Available online. URL: http://www.nytimes.com/2002/01/24/technology/drawn-to-the-hearth-s-electronic-glow.html?pagewanted=all.

La Ferla, Ruth. "Perfect Model: Gorgeous, No Complaints, Made of Pixels." *New York Times*, May 6, 2001. Available online. URL: http://www.nytimes.com/2001/05/06/style/perfect-model-gorgeous-no-complaints-made-of-pixels.html.

Olsen, Stefanie. "Advertisers Face Up to TiVo Reality." *Cnet.news*, April 26, 2004. Available online. URL: http://news.cnet.com/2100-1024_3-5200073.html.

Poor, Alfred. "LCD Monitors: Brighter, Sharper, Cheaper." *PC Magazine*, March 22, 2003. Available online. URL: http://www.pcmag.com/article2/0,2817,976572,00.asp.

Shachtman, Noah. "The Army's New Land Warrior Gear: Why Soldiers Don't Like It." *Popular Mechanics,* May 2007. Available online. URL: http://www.popularmechanics.com/technology/military_law/4215715.html?do=print.

Slotnik, Daniel E. "Cartoons of a Racist Past Lurk on YouTube." *New York Times,* April 28, 2008. Available online. URL: http://www.nytimes.com/2008/04/28/business/media/28cartoon.html.

Snider, Burr. "The Toy Story Story." *Wired,* December 1995. Available online. URL: http://www.wired.com/wired/archive/3.12/toy.story.html.

Specter, Michael. "Latest Films for $2: Video Piracy Booms in Russia." *New York Times,* April 11, 1995. Available online. URL: http://www.nytimes.com/1995/04/11/world/latest-films-for-2-video-piracy-booms-in-russia.html.

Further Resources

Books

Berners-Lee, Tim. *Weaving the Web: The Original Design and Ultimate Destiny of the World Wide Web.* New York: HarperCollins, 2000.

Campbell-Kelly, Martin and William Aspray. *Computer: A History of the Information Machine.* New York: Westview Press, 2004.

Gates, Bill. *The Road Ahead.* New York: Penguin Books, 1995.

Gregg, John R. *Ones and Zeros: Understanding Boolean Algebra, Digital Circuits, and the Logic of Sets.* New York: Wiley & Sons–IEEE, 1998.

Hafner, Katie and Matthew Lyon. *Where Wizards Stay Up Late: The Origins of the Internet.* New York: Simon & Schuster, 1996.

Jenkins, Henry. *Convergence Culture: Where Old and New Media Collide.* New York: New York University Press, 2006.

———. *Fans, Bloggers, and Gamers: Media Consumers in a Digital Age.* New York: New York University Press, 2006.

Lessig, Lawrence. *Remix: Making Art and Commerce Thrive in the Hybrid Economy.* New York: Penguin Books, 2008.

Negroponte, Nicholas. *Being Digital.* New York: Knopf, 1995.

Nye, David E. *Technology Matters: Questions to Live With.* Cambridge: Massachusetts Institute of Technology Press, 2006.

Palfrey, John and Urs Gasser. *Born Digital: Understanding the First Generation of Digital Natives.* New York: Basic Books, 2008.

Schneier, Bruce. *Secrets and Lies: Digital Security in a Networked World.* New York: Wiley & Sons, 2000.

White, Ron and Tim Downs. *How Computers Work, 8th ed.* Indianapolis: Que Publishing, 2005.

Web Sites

Centers for Disease Control and Prevention

http://www.cdc.gov

A government-run Web site that has information related to effects of computer use on health.

Central Intelligence Agency

https://www.cia.gov/library/publications/the-world-factbook

Web site of the U.S. Government intelligence agency that provides information about digital crime all over the world. The CIA Factbook is also a good source of information about different places.

Entertainment Software Association (ESA)

http://www.theesa.com

U.S. association exclusively dedicated to serving the business and public affairs needs of companies that publish computer and video games for video game consoles, personal computers, and the Internet.

Exploratorium: The Museum of Science, Art and Human Perception

http://www.exploratorium.edu

An excellent web resource containing much information on the scientific explanations of everyday things.

Geek.com

http://www.geek.com

Resource for news and developments on all aspects of digital technology.

HighDef Forum

http://www.highdefforum.com

This Web-based forum offers information related to the developments in digital and high definition video.

HowStuffWorks, Inc.
http://www.howstuffworks.com
Contains a large number of articles, generally written by knowl-edgeable authors, explaining the science behind everything from computers to electromagnetism.

Institute of Electrical and Electronics Engineers
http://www.ieee.com
International organization involved in the study of computers.

International Communication Association
http://www.icahdq.org
The association offers Web-based resources to understand how human communication works in general and in the context of digital technologies.

Interpol Cybercrime Page
http://www.interpol.int/public/TechnologyCrime/Default.asp
Contains information on the efforts Interpol, an international police organization, is making to prevent digital crime in different regions.

Library of Congress
http://www.loc.gov/index.html
This excellent Web site is a resource for doing research on many different topics using digital technology.

Motion Picture Association of America
http://www.mpaa.org
This Web site offers information on how the different digital music and video formats have evolved and explores the current issues regarding digital video and music.

Psychology Matters
http://psychologymatters.apa.org
A Web site with information on the psychological aspects of computer use.

Science Daily
http://www.sciencedaily.com
Links to information on the developments in basic science research that have an impact on the development of digital technologies.

Picture Credits

Index

Page numbers in *italics* indicate illustrations or diagrams.

About the Author

Ananda Mitra, Ph.D. is the chair of the Department of Communication at Wake Forest University. He teaches courses on technology, popular culture, issues related to South Asia, and research methods. He has been a technology commentator for regional, national, and international media, such as *Time* magazine. Mitra has published articles in leading communications journals as well as two books.

ML

8/10